STRAIGHT UP

Or

ON THE ROCKS

A

Cultural

History of

American

Drink

WILLIAM GRIMES

Simon & Schuster

New York London Toronto

Sydney Tokyo Singapore

SIMON & SCHUSTER

Simon & Schuster Building
Rockefeller Center
1230 Avenue of the Americas
New York, New York 10020

1   3   5   7   9   10   8   6   4   2

Library of Congress Cataloging-in-Publication Data

Grimes, William.
Straight up or on the rocks : a cultural history of American drink
/ William Grimes.
p.   cm.
Includes bibliographical references (p. 179) and index.
1. Cocktails.   2. Alcoholic beverages—United States—History.
I. Title.
TX951.G7864   1993
641.8'74—dc20   92-23269
                                                          CIP

ISBN: 0-671-76724-0

To Nancy

ACKNOWLEDGMENTS

Special thanks to Anita Leclerc of *Esquire*, the editor who got me started, and to Carla Glasser, who proposed the idea and stuck with it.

CONTENTS

PREFACE   *15*

1

THE MARTINI   *25*

The king of cocktails and how it grew

2

CONCEIVED IN LIBERTY   *36*

Cut loose from England, the colonial settlers find that strange ingredients are no obstacle to making a good drink

3

FIRST STIRRINGS   *49*

Heading west with whiskey on their minds, the pioneers make a remarkable discovery

Contents

4

SWINGING DOORS *67*

*In an era of opulence, the watering holes
were as ornate as the cocktails*

5

THE ICEMAN COMETH *76*

The big chill sets in, and the cocktail takes off

6

THE GOLDEN AGE CLASSICS *84*

*The cocktails that made the
quattrocento of American drink*

7

THE JAZZ AGE *93*

The booze was bad, but the speakeasies were good

8

RECONSTRUCTION *107*

America turns to the gray flannel cocktail

9

VODKA ÜBER ALLES 118

From Russia with love, the ultimate cocktail fuel

POSTSCRIPT 125

Thoughts on the future of America's greatest invention

RECIPES 133

Whiskey Cocktails **135**
Brandy Cocktails **143**
Gin Drinks **146**
Rum Drinks **156**
Champagne Drinks **162**
Vodka Drinks **165**
Tequila Drinks **169**
Wine and Vermouth Cocktails **171**
Miscellaneous **173**
Nonalcoholic Drinks **176**

BIBLIOGRAPHY 179

INDEX 184

Perhaps it's made of whiskey and perhaps it's made of gin,
Perhaps there's orange bitters and a lemon peel within,
Perhaps it's called Martini and perhaps it's called, again,
The name that spread Manhattan's fame among the sons of men;
Perhaps you like it garnished with what thinking men avoid,
The little blushing cherry that is made of celluloid,
But be these matters as they may, a cher confrère *you are*
If you admire the cocktail they pass along the bar.

Wallace Irwin, "The Great American Cocktail"
San Francisco News Letter, *March 8, 1902*

PREFACE

National genius is almost by definition indefinable. It's as likely to reside in a turn of phrase, a facial expression, or a culinary quirk as it is in the grand determining events we normally think of as history. No one would argue that the French Revolution was less than epoch-making, but France expresses its Frenchness more immediately, and just as persuasively, in a glass of burgundy or the national enthusiasm for obscure American film directors. These are the parts that add up to a much greater whole, the small but colorful fish that slip through the historian's net.

America, too, expresses its character in a thousand seemingly trivial but potent messages, unremarked upon by the natives themselves but instantly perceived by outsiders. One of them is the cocktail.

The United States could be described as the country where people mix their drinks in strange, tantalizing combinations and then consume them icy cold. It is the land of the brave and the home of the martini. This sounds flip (the name of a colonial drink, by the way). We would like the world to admire us for achievements like the Bill of Rights or the Marshall Plan. But cultural influence doesn't work that way. No one admires an abstraction. Or more precisely, the admiration one feels for an abstraction tends to be abstract; genuine emotion thrives on particulars.

For most of the world, America is the great entertainment factory, a country dedicated to life, liberty, and fun. Our economy reflects the fact: while exports of automobiles, steel, and virtually every other product fashioned by the human hand slide downward, the entertainment industry chalks up record export numbers. In 1990, it contributed a whopping $2.5 billion to the balance of payments. The New Jerusalem envisioned by the Puritans has turned out to be the world's leading manufacturer of idle amusement and cheap thrills. The Americans builded them a shining city on a hill—and they called it Disneyland. Not even the Founding Fathers can compete with the allure of pop music, Hollywood movies, or the seductive sound of ice chattering in a silver cocktail shaker. These are the tangible, consumable expressions of the Constitution's lofty principles, the free culture of a free people.

The cocktail, in other words, is something more than a mere drink. It may not be, as H. L. Mencken called it, "the greatest of all the contributions of the American way of life to the salvation of humanity," but it remains a durable, deeply appealing component of Americanness, born of experiment and ingenuity, and, like all genuine art forms, inexhaustible and infinitely adaptable. Mencken once claimed that he and a friend hired a mathematician to compute how many cocktails could be made from the ingredients available at a respectable bar. The total was 17,864,392,788. "We tried 273 at random," he reported, "and found them all good."

Thousands of new cocktails have appeared since Mencken commissioned his study. The Sage of Baltimore did not live to see the Fuzzy Navel, Sex on the Beach, or the Teeny Weeny Woo Woo. Perhaps it's just as well. But he would have understood the manic inventiveness that spawned the Slippery Nipple and others of that ilk. Christian theology holds that God created the world as an expression of the plenitude of His being. The inner logic of the cocktail is precisely the reverse. One of the first modern cultural signs, it expresses pure potentiality. It's a glass-enclosed void in which anything can happen, a restless, anxiety-tinged emptiness, forever spinning off variants. The neon martini glass, effulgent symbol of the American bar, is always empty.

This profound instability and waywardness lies at the very heart of the cocktail. It is fundamentally radical. Although historians often point out that the colonial tavern was a cradle of the Revolution, they do not mention that it was in the tavern that Americans first began disturbing the established hierarchies of wine and spirits, mixing and fixing with whatever alcoholic and flavoring materials lay ready to hand, gradually evolving a purely American notion of the drink.

The potations of the Old World, seemingly as ancient as root and soil, reflected an immutable social order and the attendant values of homogeneity, cohesion, and tradition. They still do. European efforts to break loose and embrace the cocktail have always been self-consciously American—witness *le bar américain*—and less than convincing. The spirit may be willing, but when it comes to fundamental matters like drink, national currents run strong and deep. The poet Paul Claudel once remarked that "a cocktail is to a glass of wine as rape is to love." It's hard to break the hold of a sentiment like that.

Small wonder, then, that Europe has always taken an academic approach to the cocktail, as though it were a compelling but ultimately inscrutable artifact, like an African mask. In 1973, a bartender at the Savoy Hotel in London decided to celebrate England's entry into the EEC with a Common Market Cocktail: equal parts Elixir d'Anu (Belgium), cherry brandy (Denmark), dry vermouth (France), Schlichte (West Germany), sloe gin (Great Britain), curaçao (the Netherlands), dry white wine (Luxembourg), coffee liqueur (Ireland),

and Carpano (Italy). Needless to say, this nightmare of pedantry was served in the hotel's "American" bar, and it's a safe bet that no customer in his right mind has ever ordered one. The Common Market Cocktail is a set of bureaucratic guidelines, not a drink.

You can't blame Europe for trying. Wherever it has made an appearance, the cocktail has had a beneficial, loosening effect on rigid social customs. Alec Waugh, brother of Evelyn, described the cocktail's incursion into England in the 1920s, at a time when the awkward period of predinner socializing was known as the *mauvais quart d'heure*. The cocktail came as a godsend, and Britain's flaming youth grabbed for it with both hands, especially when it appeared in the guise of the champagne cocktail. (For the results, consult the novels of Evelyn Waugh, passim.) But as with jazz, appreciation never led to inventiveness. Professional bartenders' organizations were formed, but in spirit they lay somewhere between a medieval craft guild and the Académie Française. On occasion, they sponsored tournaments of skill, resulting in champion cocktails every bit as good as the Savoy's Common Market.

Americans have approached the cocktail much as they have such popular art forms as the cartoon or the Tin Pan Alley song, driven by imagination, exuberance, and the profit motive. From the beginning, there has been a tendency to err on the side of excess. The flashy, vulgar drink has always been with us. True to the Hollywood ratio, there are one hundred execrable cocktails for every classic. But without the awful drinks, the classics wouldn't exist. And the classics could not have been invented anywhere else but in the United States.

This has something to do with a peculiarity of American society that Europeans dimly perceive but cannot fully understand. The free-and-easy, gregarious American social style disguises a profound detachment and sense of solitude. The surface warmth that foreigners never fail to remark upon belies a coolness within. This is part of the Faustian bargain that America has made to gain freedom and riches. Turning their back on Europe, the colonists chose to breathe a freer, harsher air. Along with the constraints that made the villages and towns of the Old World deadly and claustrophobic, they threw off the warm blanket of custom, family ties, friendships, and loyalties. Competitive and mobile, Americans have had to develop social forms that promote quick and effortless acquaintance rather than strong, lasting ties. In no other society are strangers who have grown up thousands of miles apart more likely to be thrown together and expected not only to get along and do business but to regard each other as friends. Hence the cocktail party, more often than not a gathering of near strangers brought together in a setting of false intimacy.

The cocktail stands for sociability with no strings attached. It is shallow. But it is also profound. It evokes the solitary man at the end of the bar, lost in his own thoughts, staring into the plumbless depths of a three-ounce glass.

Cold, clean, slightly astringent, the cocktail represents a decisive break with the preindustrial past, when liquors were seen as a kind of food and prized for their warming, nourishing properties. Falstaff's red nose and enormous belly testified to the combustive, nutritive powers of ale and sack. Smollett's roisterers rallied round the silver bowl brimming with fumacious, scalding punch; Boswell and Johnson found inspiration in their nightly two-bottle ration of viscous port. Santa Claus, a deep appreciator of the boiling punch bowl, is a potbellied stove in human form: face aflame, red clothes blazing. Heat, fat, solidity, and weight—these are the key Old World attributes, as ancient as the caveman, for whom fire meant food, warmth, safety, and companionship.

Consider one of the great cocktail drinkers of our time, James

Bond. Although patriotic, Bond is in fundamental respects un-English. The first Transatlantic Man, he is perfectly at home with advanced technology, flashy gadgetry, and foreign languages. The contrast with postwar Britain could not be more stark. Significantly, Bond asserts his identity through highly chilled, distinctive cocktails. He even invents his own. M., his boss, sticks to whiskey at his tweedy club, Blades. Bond's peculiar drinking tastes are as alien as his fast cars, faster women, and razor-sharp suits. With his vodka martini, Bond announces, in effect, "I am modern, therefore American."

The triumph of the cocktail did not come overnight. Like the United States itself, it began as an Anglo-American hybrid, struggled to find a native form, achieved full maturity in the late nineteenth century, and today flourishes thanks to myriad international influences, most of them from the third world. As the cocktail goes, so goes the nation.

And vice versa. The cocktail has now entered a more thoughtful, reflective, even self-conscious phase, the result of moderated drinking habits. To the despair of distillers, Americans, already a rather abstemious people, are drinking less. The downward trend began a decade ago and shows no sign of abating. Law and public opinion now take a harsh view of drunken driving, and rightly so. Public intoxication no longer seems quite so amusing as it did twenty or thirty years ago. A health-conscious population regards the now almost mythic three-martini lunch with mingled horror and awe. *Three martinis?* What race of giants roamed the land in those far-off days? Easier to picture Paul Bunyan felling an ox with one fist. Today's business lunch is lubricated with a Perrier and a slice of lime; in a wild mood, the modern executive might order a glass of chilled chardonnay.

Somewhat paradoxically, moderation seems to have inspired a kind of connoisseurship. Even as consumption declines, interest in the fine points of wine and spirits has picked up, if only for practical reasons. If you're going to drink less, why not drink better? And if you're going to drink better—to move up from *cru bourgeois* to second growth, from blended Scotch to a recherché single malt from Jura—doesn't it pay to know more about what you're pouring into the glass? Knowledge has a way of feeding on its own appetite, and soon natural curiosity takes over. Where did the Bronx and the sidecar come from? What on earth was a Zaza cocktail? Were martinis always dry? How did they get to be called martinis in the first place? This book grew out of questions like these, and the notion that even if firm answers proved hard to come by, the search would allow for some creative browsing along the way.

The cocktail sounds like a wily game bird. It acts like one too. It can be glimpsed only fleetingly, at the margins of history, where it lives a flickering, elusive existence, turning up in the short descriptive passage of a traveler, the offhand remark of a fictional character, the unembellished report of a journalist. As the temperance movement gained ascendancy in the United States, references to drink, other than as a social evil, virtually disappeared from the printed record. American writers, notorious for their bibulous ways, rarely thought of the ever-present glass in their hand as an object worthy of notice, a piece of social information as revealing as clothing style, accent, or occupation. The cocktail has been, so to speak, everywhere and nowhere, a minor actor on the stage of history but one whose story deserves to be told before it disappears forever. Back in the 1930s, G. Selmer Fougner used to issue "calls" for cocktail recipes in his "Along the Wine Trail" column for the *New York Sun*. On one occasion, four hundred readers responded to his request for the correct ingredients in a Ward 8. Today, perhaps half that number of Americans even know that the Ward 8 is a drink.

A sense of history also pervades the book's recipe section, which reflects a rigorous winnowing-out process. Most cocktails, like most plays or paintings, are bad. The standard cocktail guides ignore this sad fact. The encyclopedic approach makes sense in a book intended for professional bartenders, but for the rest of mankind, profusion means confusion. This book includes over a hundred recipes, selected according to the principle of benevolent elitism. It presents the classics and worthy variations thereon, as well as deserving drinks that have inexplicably fallen out of favor over the decades. In other words, breeding counts. But talent does too. The American cocktail is nothing if not forward-looking and optimistic. Accordingly, the winner's circle of drinks includes a goodly number of new and innovative cocktails served at America's best bars, hotels, and restaurants. The door slams shut, however, on the flashy newcomer—the fellow with the loud suit and the back-slapping manner. He will be directed to that singles bar down the road, where the drinks come in fun colors and go out of fashion in a week.

What makes a great cocktail? For that matter, what is a cocktail? The word first appears in 1806, conveniently enough in the form of a definition. The editor of the Hudson, New York, *Balance and Columbian Repository*, responding to a perplexed reader's query, wrote: "Cocktail is a stimulating liquor, composed of spirits of any kind, sugar, water, and bitters." Substitute ice for water, and the definition holds up pretty well. But even the slimmest of cocktail books will contain numerous exceptions. Consistent with the negative logic of the cocktail, any drink merits the name that cannot be proven *not* to be a cocktail. Those with the taste for scholastic argument can parse the differences between a cocktail and an aperitif, but that way madness lies. By the rules, a Manhattan is a cocktail, not a before-dinner appetite enhancer, but in practice Americans drink all sorts of things before, during, and after a meal and would probably call them all cocktails as long as they were cold and had some spirit as a base. "Cocktail" and "mixed drink" have often been synonymous, yet cocktails have on occasion been pared down to a single ingredient. So: Scotch with ice cubes—yes. A white wine with ice cubes—no. Jell-O Shots—vodka-laced cubes of flavored gelatin served in a little paper cup—no, no, no.

Abominations like the Jell-O Shot remind us that standards do matter. Reason and custom suggest that a cocktail should be cold, snappy, invigorating to the palate, and pleasing to the eye. That covers most of the territory. A rare few, like the daiquiri and the martini, combine their minimal ingredients to achieve, through a magical synthesis, an entirely new flavor. Others are content to play beguiling variations on a theme. Still others, like the highball, don't do much of anything at all but nevertheless have their humble place in the grand scheme.

Whatever a cocktail's ingredients, the whole should add up to more than the sum of the parts. And the parts should coexist in a tensile balance—what the old Charles Atlas ads called "Dynamic Tension." No one ingredient should overpower the others: The bartender who pours with a heavy hand does no service to the drinker if the entire cocktail is thereby thrown out of joint.

A good cocktail, properly mixed, should lift the spirits, refresh the mind, and put into healthy perspective the countless worries and grievances of modern life. The fretful neurotic who shakes up an after-work martini should emerge from the experience a changed human being: more generous and sociable, inclined toward deeper thought and the pleasures of the imagination. In that mood, Martini

Preface

Man might perhaps spare a thought for the anonymous tavernkeepers and bartenders of the past three hundred fifty years, the humble inventors who brought to perfection this unheralded branch of the culinary arts. America has given the world much. It should take pride in the cocktail too.

THE MARTINI

1

There is a point at which the marriage
of gin and vermouth is consummated.
It varies a little with the constituents,
but for a gin of 94.4 proof and a harmonious
vermouth it may be generalized as about 3.7 to one.

–Bernard DeVoto, The Hour (1946)

Human invention has launched untold thousands of cocktails, but only one has developed a genuine mystique: the martini. It is the quintessential cocktail, the standard by which all others are judged. Immune to shifting taste and fashion, the martini not only has endured—it has prospered. The Jack Rose, the sidecar, the Bronx, where are they now? Those tasty mainstays of the 1930s and 1940s survive only as period pieces. Yet the martini maintains its steady course, a blue-chip investment paying out the same handsome dividend year after year.

Let the martini serve as a touchstone for this book, a north star by which to navigate the bewildering world of mixed drinks. And just as surveys of Western art begin with an inspirational discourse on the

Acropolis, let this rambling, digressive tour of American drink start with the undisputed model of cocktail perfection.

For the true martini believer, the combination of gin, vermouth, and olive is the Holy Trinity. And like any theological principle, it has given rise to doctrinal dispute. Put two worshipers in the same room and the arguments begin. Points of contention include, but are not limited to, the proper ingredients and their ideal proportions, the fastest way to achieve maximum coldness, and the merits of shaking versus stirring. Should a glass pitcher or a metal shaker be used? Should the olive have a pimiento or not? These are matters of faith, not reason, for the martini is a religion. It even has its martyr: Sherwood Anderson, who succumbed to peritonitis after swallowing the toothpick from a martini olive. Consider him a sacrifice to the Egyptian god of thirst, Dri Mart Ini, whose cult was discovered by "Percival Slathers" in the *New York Sun* seventy-five years ago. According to the columnist, ancient artists depicted the god as a priest of Isis, "shaking a drink in a covered urn of glass while the 15th pharaoh of the dynasty of Lush is shown with protruding cottony tongue quivering with pleasurable expectation."

Just how the drink got its name remains a mystery. And trying to solve it leads the hapless etymologist down one of the most meandering, aimless paths that the English language can offer. The British assume it originated with the Martini & Henry rifle, used throughout the empire and known for its strong kick. The Italians assume, plausibly enough, that the name comes from Martini & Rossi vermouth. Both of them are wrong.

So are most Americans, but somewhat more interestingly, they are wrong in two different ways. Over the years, two schools of thought on the time and place of the martini's origin have evolved, which, for convenience, we can label the West and the East Coast theories. Let us consider each in turn.

The West Coast theory, to make matters more complicated, divides into two subtheories, the San Francisco and the Martinez. The former holds that the renowned bartender Jerry Thomas mixed the first martini at San Francisco's Occidental Hotel in the 1860s for a traveler who said he was bound for nearby Martinez, hence the name. Partisans of the latter say that the world's first martini drinker was a gold miner in the 1870s who dropped by the Martinez bar of Julio [sic] Richelieu, a French immigrant, to buy a bottle of whiskey. Since the gold nugget he used to pay for it was worth a little more than the whiskey, the miner demanded his change in the form of a cocktail. He got a new one, instantly dubbed the Martinez.

Both West Coast theories rest on sand. For one thing, the Martinez cocktail first makes its appearance, not in Jerry Thomas's book, but in an 1884 bar book by O. H. Byron, who describes it as a Manhattan in which gin is substituted for whiskey. If Thomas invented the drink, he mysteriously omitted it from the 1862 edition of his *Bar-tender's Guide*, subtitled *The Bon-Vivant's Companion*, America's first cocktail book. Not until the 1887 edition does it make an appearance—and consider the recipe: one dash of bitters, two dashes of maraschino, one wineglass (!) of vermouth, two small lumps of ice, and one ounce of Old Tom gin, with sugar syrup to be added on request.

Is this really a martini? True, there's vermouth, but Thomas had in mind the sweet red Italian variety. There's gin, but again, it's the wrong kind. Old Tom gin, a rarity nowadays, has sugar added during distillation. Jerry Thomas's cocktail is little more than a molten gumdrop. Much closer to the mark is Thomas's 1862 recipe for a gin cocktail, which calls for gin, curaçao, bitters, and gum syrup, garnished with a twist of lemon.

The East Coast theory holds that Martini di Arma di Taggia, a bartender at the Knickerbocker Hotel in New York, created a drink using equal parts gin and dry vermouth sometime after arriving in America in 1912. That date would seem to make di Taggia a straggler in the race, since several bar books from the period 1880 to 1900 include martini recipes. But wait! These early martinis, like Jerry Thomas's Martinez, envisioned Italian vermouth. So di Taggia could be the man. On the other hand, William F. Mulhall, a veteran bartender, wrote of serving martinis at New York's swank Hoffman House back in the 1880s, and although he did not specify the ingredients, he did refer to both sweet and dry martinis.

By today's standards, which call for one part vermouth to anywhere between five and fifteen parts gin, the Knickerbocker martini was sickly sweet, but it definitely bears the distinctive markings of the cocktail. After all, a ratio of three to one was typical as recently as the 1930s, when *Esquire* was recommending Italian vermouth for a medium martini, and equal parts Italian and French vermouth for a semidry. One of the great cultural shocks still achievable in this age of jet travel and global communications is to order a martini in a British pub. The wretch who makes this mistake will receive a small glass of sweet vermouth. A request for a dry martini will elicit a small glass of French vermouth. The fail-safe method is to ask for a "gin and French" with ice.

Gradually, the martini became drier. Somewhere along the way it achieved greatness. As *New Yorker* readers cannot help but know, the drink (like the magazine) has for decades been a kind of tribal totem for the East Coast business establishment, the Wall Street–Madison Avenue nexus. Its power as a symbol lives on, well past the era of its actual dominance. A characteristic cartoon in a recent issue of the magazine showed two cavemen, returning from the hunt, carrying giant olives toward a giant martini glass. But the martini's fame extends far beyond the traditional WASP watering holes. The triangular glass with an olive in it has been adopted as the international symbol for "bar." It's the only cocktail that has made the leap from drink to symbol.

It's also the only cocktail to have inspired books. Lowell Edmunds, a classics professor at Rutgers University, produced a treatise devoted entirely to the martini, *The Silver Bullet*. The book, an ideal blend of careful scholarship, ingenuity, and enthusiasm, explores the "ambiguities" of the martini. The martini is at once civilized and uncivilized, connoting sophistication but also excess. It is sensitive yet tough—susceptible to "bruising," it is more delicate than nitroglycerin and nearly as potent.

The most beguiling of the ambiguities that Edmunds finds in the martini is its ability to be at once classic and individual, public and private. As a two-ingredient drink, it should logically have a set form pleasing to all martini drinkers; yet it seems to demand endless tinkering and fosters a thousand idiosyncrasies. Every martini devotee believes he has a particular variant or technical refinement that makes the drink his own, yet it always remains a martini. The reason for this is not hard to find. The martini inclines the mind toward meditation, and meditation promotes a deep personal bond between drinker and drink.

In his autobiography, the film director Luis Buñuel spoke of his need to induce a state of reverie by sitting alone in a cool, dark bar, drinking martinis. He insisted, quite seriously, that the cocktail played a "primordial role" in his life. Like all martini drinkers, he offered his own technique, which requires putting glass, shaker, and gin in the refrigerator a day ahead of time: "Then pour a few drops of Noilly Prat and half a demitasse spoon of Angostura bitters over the ice. Shake it, then pour it out, keeping only the ice, which retains a faint taste of both. Then pour straight gin over the ice, shake it again and serve."

FDR's martinis show a similar quirkiness. Stalin downed one at the Teheran Conference, pronouncing it very good but "cold on the stomach." He was being polite. Roosevelt's recipe, provided by his secretary to a persistent radio reporter named Jack Reed, called for two parts gin to one part vermouth, with a teaspoon of olive brine. It was served with an olive and, "for extra smoothness," the rim of the glass was rubbed with lemon peel. The result was noisome but perhaps diplomatically effective, since one administration official characterized U.S.-Soviet relations under Roosevelt as the "four martinis and let's have an agreement" era.

The personal approach in martini mixing tends to elicit an equal and opposite countertheory. Always, an expert is on hand. Paul Farley, in John O'Hara's *Butterfield 8*, says he'd "always taken a holy delight in not bruising a poor little cocktail" but was converted by a contemptuous English bartender. "He told me a Martini ought to be shaken very hard, briskly, a few vigorous shakes up and down, so that the gin and vermouth would be cracked into a proper *foamy* mixture." The alleged advantage here is that the drink becomes aerated and hence less potent, making it possible to polish off several.

This is pure nonsense. Try shaking a martini. Shake it for an hour, if you like, and see if anything like foam results. It doesn't. O'Hara's martini is a literary artifact, the direct descendant of the martini with "the smooth infinitesimal foam" that makes a cameo appearance in John Dos Passos's *Manhattan Transfer*.

Edmunds also found in the martini a number of unambiguous messages: It is American. It is urban, upper class, and male. It is nostalgic. It is cold, dry, pure, clear. "It is a simple, strict, one might say puritanical, drink. Its pleasure, which is not voluptuous but astringent, can only be expressed by oxymoron—sensuous coldness, opulent dryness, mysterious clarity, alluring purity." This is the martini that Hemingway's Frederic Henry responds to in *A Farewell to Arms*, when he says, "I had never tasted anything so cool and clean. They made me feel civilized."

It could also be argued that the martini is capitalist. It is the official drink of America's business class, the high-octane fuel that powered Wall Street and Madison Avenue well into the 1970s, when the age of Perrier and lime began. A left-leaning social critic might propose that these professions, involving more than the usual moral compromises required by adult life, find their antidote in the martini, whose clarity and purity represent the uncorrupted soul of the corrupt man, just as the preppy look pays homage to youthful idealism and physical grace. In a world built on compromise, the businessman can insist with utter fanaticism on the martini as he likes it, *demands* it: drier than dry.

Vermouth is therefore a contaminating yet indispensable element, even if—or especially if—it is not used at all. The rejection of the vermouth is an essential part of the martini ritual, a rite of purification. "The affliction that is cutting down the productive time in the office and destroying the benign temper of most bartenders is the thing called the *very* dry martini," the *New York Times* said in 1952. "It's a mass madness, a cult, a frenzy, a body of folklore, a mystique, an *expertise* of a sort which may very well earn for this decade the name of the Numb (or Glazed) 50s." (Curiously, on Madison Avenue, the martini was referred to, depending on the garnish, as deep-dish olive, lemon, or onion pie.)

The *Times* account noted that at one midtown bar, martinis were being listed as dry, very dry, and extra dry, with an additional dime tacked on at each step. There is no reason why three or four even drier categories could not have been added on, since, past a certain point, dryness becomes a notion rather than a taste sensation. Many a bartender has served up an icy glass of pure gin, only to have it returned with the angry demand, "Make it again—but dry this time!" Schenley Distillers once tried to capitalize on the trend by launching a product called The Naked Martini. It was pure gin, cut to 80 proof, the idea being that this would approximate the taste of a no-vermouth martini slightly diluted by ice cubes.

In the heyday of the martini, the 1950s, the merest suspicion of wetness could trigger a righteous wrath. The archetypal martini drinker of the magazine cartoons and a thousand popular jokes seethes with a barely repressed anger; he's an overworked, deeply frustrated yes-man who buries his principles at work but draws the line when it comes to his martini. In a joke from the great martini decade, a businessman asks his bartender for a martini with twenty-five parts gin to one part vermouth. "Would you like a twist of lemon with that?" the bartender inquires. "When I want a goddam lemonade, I'll ask for it," the martini man snarls. There are two things worth noting about the joke. First, only a martini cultist would find it funny. Second, it assumes that an explosion of rage is the appropriate response to the desecration of a dry martini.

Martini lore abounds in fanciful ways to reject vermouth. It's enough to pass the cork over the bottle and whisper "vermouth," or to expose the glass to the label on the vermouth bottle. As detective Nick Charles in the "Thin Man" movies, William Powell used a medicine dropper to eke out the vermouth, an approach that was improved on when the vermouth atomizer was invented. Progress continues to be made in this area, and the serious martini drinker can now order vermouth-soaked olives by mail.

No religion can exist without heresy, and the martini has witnessed more than its share. In 1951, a Chicago liquor dealer held a contest for variations on the martini and received two hundred entries. The twenty-five finalists included sauternes and Scotch martinis, a liebfraumilch martini, and a recipe that called for a sliced clove of garlic to be rubbed around the rim of the glass. The winner was a martini served in a glass rinsed with Cointreau and garnished with an anchovy-stuffed olive. In 1959, a Washington, D.C., bar achieved momentary fame by promoting the "dillytini": a martini containing a string bean that had been marinated in dill vinegar. The same year, a Chicago restaurateur by the name of Morton C. Morton triumphantly announced the invention of the Mortini: mix two fifths of gin and one ounce of vermouth; add a peeled Bermuda onion. The drink, said Morton, was enjoyed "only by people with the most fashionable psychoses."

For a time, in the late 1960s and the 1970s, the martini went into steep decline. Younger drinkers, seduced by Boone's Farm wine or marijuana, did not seem to be replenishing the ranks. The young bloods of the day, in full revolt against everything their fathers stood for, would no sooner have ordered a martini than they would have rung doorbells for Richard Nixon. "Young people do not like martinis and they're not drinking them. Ever! Anywhere!" James Villas wrote in *Esquire* in 1973, assessing the martini mood among the young. "Generally, the martini signifies absolute decadence. Specifically it means a bitter, medicinal-tasting beverage. It stands for everything from phony bourgeois values and social snobbery to jaded alcoholism and latent masochism."

Because young people were not drinking martinis, journalists and other nervous trend-watchers assumed that the drink was dead. But Villas conducted a little experiment. He sat down in the Oak Room Bar at the Plaza Hotel and watched its two bartenders at work. They served up about five hundred cocktails during the afternoon rush. About three hundred were martinis, both vodka and gin, drunk by men over thirty. In other words, demographics were on the side of the martini. An aging and prospering baby boom generation would sooner or later find its way back to gin and vermouth.

It took a while. As late as 1985, *Time* magazine called the martini an "amusing antique." But in the past few years, as rampant nostalgia has set in for the elegance of the thirties—or at least Hollywood's version of it—the martini has staged a comeback. Suddenly, the martini seems rather hip.

The aesthetic pull is not hard to understand. Despite its nineteenth-century origins, the martini has become fixed in the popular imagination as a 'deco drink. It harks back to the surge of optimistic modernism when the bold, clean lines of the Bauhaus, de Stijl, and the new industrial design set the pulse racing. The classic martini glass, a simple, minimalist geometric form, ranks as one of the enduring legacies of modernism.

Something strange yet perhaps predictable has happened to the martini. Vodka has supplanted gin. The "purer" vodka has staked its claim and triumphed. According to the American Bartenders Association, vodka now goes into two out of every three martinis, although bartenders still assume that a customer ordering a martini *tout court* has gin in mind. The logic of the martini has turned the drink inside out. It now glows in perfect transparency—sans vermouth, sans botanicals, sans everything.

It is pleasing to think that the first Americans, adherents of a fierce, uncompromising faith, would recognize the vodka martini as their own. It is a Puritan drink, and it is to the Puritans that we now turn, the intolerant progenitors of a free and tolerant society, enemies of frivolity who laid the foundations for that most frivolous of American creations, the cocktail.

CONCEIVED IN LIBERTY

2

If barley be wanting to make into malt,
We must be content and think it no fault,
For we can make liquor to sweeten our lips,
Of pumpkins, and parsnips, and walnut-tree chips.

—Anonymous, 1630s

Our Puritan forefathers arrived on the shores of New England with a passion for freedom and a raging thirst. When the Pilgrims dropped anchor at Plymouth Rock, it was no coincidence that the liquor supply was getting low. William Bradford, anxiously scanning the rocky shoreline of Massachusetts, decided not to "take time for further search or consideration, our victuals being much spent, especially our Beere." This was no joking matter. The *Mayflower* had brought along a cooper for the express purpose of tending the precious kegs: none other than John Alden, who later found gainful employment in "The Courtship of Miles Standish."

The early settlers thought long and hard about securing adequate supplies of liquid refreshment before leaving the old country. When

John Winthrop, first governor of the Massachusetts Bay Colony, set sail to America on the *Arabella,* his stores included 10,000 gallons of beer, 120 hogsheads of malt for brewing, and 12 gallons of "hot waters." That was the official supply. Just in case, most families brought their own backup barrels.

The colonists, to put it mildly, were no teetotalers. The word did not exist until the temperance movement of the early nineteenth century. The concept didn't exist, either. In their war on sensory pleasure, the Puritans never considered attacking beer and wine as inherently harmful. Gross intoxication, of course, was sinful, and Increase Mather fulminated against the habit of excessive toasting in *Wo to Drunkards* (1673). But no one condemned alcohol outright. One might as well rail against bread as a cause of gluttony. Good drink was a gift of God, a source of good cheer, the seal of friendship. Even more, drink was regarded as a kind of food, a sustaining and strength-giving substance. No worker could be expected to toil throughout the day without alcoholic fortification.

Water was the liquid of last resort, a carrier of disease, and the colonists regarded the gurgling streams of the New World with a suspicious eye. Although William Wood, of the Massachusetts Bay Company, gave high marks to the American product, finding it to be "not so sharp, but of a fatter substance, and of a more jetty colour" than in England, he still balked: "I dare not prefer it before good Beere, as some have done." For the early settlers, it was imperative to ensure a steady supply of drink.

The obstacles were formidable. European vines failed to take in the New World, and the eastern seaboard was ill suited to the grain needed to brew beer or distill alcohol. As a result, wine and brandy, as well as most beer and porter—beer's richer, darker cousin—had to be imported. In Boston, ships laden with fish and barrel staves set sail for the Canaries and Azores, where casks were banged together and filled up with wine for the return journey. The cod-for-wine business flourished, so much so that as early as 1645, the Massachusetts General Court found it worthwhile to establish duties on madeira and sherry, as well as such now forgotten favorites as bastard (a sweet Spanish wine, made from the bastardo grape), malaga (a sweet fortified wine made in Audalusia), canary (the now extinct sherry of the Canary Islands), tent (from the Spanish *tinto*, or red), and alicante (a robust red from Spain's Mediterranean coast).

Madeira was far and away the favorite wine of the colonies, in part because it traveled well, but also for economic reasons. Because of its non-European origin (the Portuguese island of Madeira is geographically part of Africa), madeira did not have to be transferred to English ships, as was required of virtually all other goods by the Trade and Navigation Acts. That made it cheaper, and wildly popular. So pronounced was the taste for madeira that as late as the 1830s, the Astor House hotel in New York offered forty-two varieties on its wine list.

Ever alert for new ways to squeeze money out of the colonies, the British clamped down with the Revenue Act of 1764. The law slapped a stiff tax on wines from Madeira and the Azores, and set low duties on Spanish and Portuguese wines. The idea was to encourage consumption of port, whose trade went through Britain, fattening the British treasury in the process. If the colonists insisted on drinking madeira, well, let them pay for it. The British would win either way.

But the colonists did not cooperate. The more idealistic of them immediately organized a boycott of taxed goods, with Yale College well in the vanguard. This early instance of campus radicalism earned warm applause from patriotic folk. "All Gentlemen of Taste, who visit the College," said the *New York Gazette*, "will think themselves better entertained with a good glass of Beer or Cider, offered them upon such principles, than they could be with the best Punch or Madeira." The more practical solution, however, was smuggling, and at this the colonists were past masters. In one official report to the Customs Board, it was noted that thirty vessels arriving at New York from Madeira and the Azores did not enter enough goods to fill even one ship. Even the dimmest-witted customs clerk could figure out what had made up the difference.

After madeira, the most popular wines were canary, port, sherry, malaga, and fayal (from the island of the same name in the Azores). French wines, especially from Bordeaux, could be found on the best tables, most notably Thomas Jefferson's, where guests could enjoy not only the best of bordeaux, burgundy, and champagne, but southern French wines from Roussillon, Provence, Frontignan, and Limoux; sauternes from the fabled Château d'Yquem; and, most unusual, Montepulciano from Italy. According to his slave Isaac, Jefferson also kept on hand some fine twelve-year-old rum from Antigua.

Imports were fine for the gentry, but they could not possibly satisfy popular demand. No, the colonists would have to develop their own indigenous resources. And they set about the task with a will. By 1629, Virginia had two brewhouses; Boston had its first malthouse in 1637. The first grain (probably corn or rye) was distilled into alcohol on Staten Island in 1640, by Willem Kieft, director general of the colony of New Netherland. Mead and metheglin, or fermented honey, were made throughout the colonies. On a small scale, the colonies tried to reproduce the drinks of the Old World.

Very soon, though, the need to improvise became apparent. Since ingredients for the traditional beverages were not always available, whatever grew locally was pressed into service. Thwarted in one direction, the colonial farmer turned to anything that would ferment, displaying the can-do spirit that would later pull America through Prohibition. St. John de Crèvecoeur, in his *Journey into Northern Pennsylvania and the State of New York*, reported that ingenious farmers were making beer from pine chips, pine buds, hemlock, fir needles, roasted corn, dried apple skins, sassafras roots, and bran. He could have added parsnips, currants, and elderberries as well. In Virginia, according to Governor William Berkeley, "The poorer sort brew their beer with molasses and bran; with Indian corn malted with drying in a stove; with persimmons dried in a cake and baked; with potatoes with the green stalks of Indian corn cut small and bruised, with pompions" (i.e., pumpkins). Last and least esteemed for beer-making purposes, according to Berkeley, was the Jerusalem arti-choke. Spruce beer, made by adding spruce twigs to malt for extra flavor, formed part of the soldier's ration. John Winthrop, Jr., the governor of Connecticut, brewed beer from corn, an achievement that won him election to the Royal Society of London. Peaches and pears were used to make their own ciders, known as peachy and perry. Peaches were also distilled into brandy, especially in the South.

Wherever apples grew (English seed had been introduced to America by 1630), cider became popular, eclipsing beer in New England by the middle of the seventeenth century. John Josselyn, who left records of two voyages to New England, in 1638 and 1663, enjoyed cider spiced and sweetened with sugar in the taphouses of Boston. He also recommended the following embellished version: "Take of Malago-Raisins, stamp them and put milk to them in a Hippocras bag and let it drain out of itself, put a quantity of this with a spoonful or two of Syrup of Clove-Gilliflowers into every bottle when you bottle your Cyder." (Hippocras, a kind of cordial made by spicing wine and passing it through a cone-shaped cloth strainer, was a medieval favorite, mentioned by Chaucer in *The Canterbury Tales*; for reasons unknown, its invention was attributed to Hippocrates.)

Cider became synonymous with good, honest living and a lack of pretense. John Adams enjoyed a full tankard before breakfast every morning. In the 1840 presidential campaign, cider even became a political issue. The Democratic candidate, Martin Van Buren, was painted by the Whigs as a sissified drinker of wines, up to and including champagne, while William Henry Harrison was marketed to the voters as a humble son of the soil, born in a log cabin and best pleased with the rustic life. One campaign song went:

> *Let Van from his coolers of silver drink wine,*
> *And lounge on his cushioned settee;*
> *Our man on his buckeye bench can recline,*
> *Content with hard cider is he.*

Cider symbolism played a major role in this, the first media-dominated campaign. Political America turned its rude hand to the art of image manipulation, with remarkable results: in a matter of months, nearly all the more repellent characteristics of modern presidential contests sprouted and achieved full maturity. In the House of Representatives, a New Hampshire Democrat, recalling the campaign, remarked acidly that "no Whig gentleman considered himself properly adorned with the ensigns of his party, unless he carried a cane with a miniature hard cider barrel for its head, or an umbrella similarly adorned."

For an extra-proof drink, New Englanders put their cider outdoors in cold weather, waited for it to freeze, and then skimmed off the ice. An improvement on this rough-and-ready method came in 1698, when a Scottish distiller named William Laird settled in Monmouth County,

New Jersey, and began turning out apple brandy, or applejack. (The distillery one of his descendants founded one hundred years later, Laird and Company of Scobeyville, today makes more than 95 percent of the applejack in the United States.) By the 1830s, nearly four hundred distilleries in Laird's state were producing "Jersey lightning," enjoyed straight or in such winter warmers as scotchem—applejack, boiling water, and a dab of mustard.

The preeminent spirit of the colonies, however, was rum. Columbus had brought sugarcane cuttings to Hispaniola on his second voyage, in 1493. The plant throve, and it did not take long for planters to discover a use for the cane that was left over after the sugar was extracted from it. In 1651, an anonymous account of Barbados noted that "the chief fudling they make in the island is Rumbullion, alias Kill-Devil, and this is made of sugar cane distilled, a hot, hellish, and terrible liquor."

Soon the colonies began trading with the West Indies, and the reign of rum began. As the standard histories once had it, rum formed one side of the "triangle trade" between America, the West Indies, and Africa. Slaves from Africa were exchanged in the West Indies for molasses, which was then brought to New England and distilled into rum. New England ships would then transport rum to West Africa and trade it for slaves, who worked the sugarcane fields that yielded the molasses. Recent scholarship has exposed the triangle-trade theory, which enjoyed currency for more than a century, as pure myth. The slave trade never counted for much in New England's economy.

But rum did. By 1763, New England had 159 rum distilleries. Boston alone had thirty, and nearly a thousand sailing vessels traded in rum out of the city. From Philadelphia northward, the distillation of rum was the leading manufacturing process.

So many of New England's rum distilleries were clustered around the town of Medford, about six miles northwest of Boston, that "Medford rum" became a kind of generic term—a much more plausible one than "stinkibus," a pungent bit of slang for the common man's choice. Although it is true that before his famous ride, Paul Revere took refuge in the home of Isaac Hall, captain of the Medford Minute Men and a distiller, there is no reason to believe the legend that he downed a few quick ones for the road.

Much of the drinking in early America took place in public houses. The colonial tavern, originally known as an "ordinary," was hotel, saloon, and municipal building all in one. To the traveler, it offered room and board. In the days before courthouses and town halls, it gave public officials a place to conduct business, with the town's freemen footing the bill. Mail was delivered and distributed at the tavern, and on militia training days, court days, and election days, its welcoming doors beckoned. When rebellion began to brew in the colonies, strategy sessions were held over a tankard at the local. It did not take long for the tavern to rival the church as a social institution. The home of good cheer and warming drinks, it offered fellowship and entertainment, even gambling. Billiards and bowling were on offer, as well as shuffleboard and cards. In the South, cockfighting and bull-baiting pulled in the crowds. Traveling players often used the tavern as a rehearsal hall. Auctions were held at taverns, as well as dances.

The tavern was the natural showcase for acrobats, conjurers, and curiosities of every sort. Exotic beasts could always be counted on to draw a crowd hungry for self-education. One advertisement offered: "A *beautiful* MOOSE. The curious in natural history are invited to Major King's Tavern, where it is to be seen a fine young moose of 16 hands in height, and well-proportioned. The properties of this fleet and tractable animal are such as will give pleasure and satisfaction to every beholder." Polar bears and performing apes also went on tour.

But few acts could compete with "the Female Sampson," who lay prone between two chairs, supporting a three-hundred-pound anvil that two men struck with sledgehammers.

As the natural forum for political debate, the tavern offered mental stimulation as well. On occasion, formal battles of wits were held. In 1756, two contestants in Massachusetts, Jonathan Gower of Lynn and Joseph Emerson of Reading, met by arrangement at a local tavern to engage in intellectual struggle. History, alas, has left no record of the verbal cut and thrust. We know only that Gower retired in defeat, vanquished by Emerson, whose wit, according to one spectator, "was beyond all human imagination."

The tone was not always so elevated. Perhaps more typical was the experience of Sarah Knight, a Boston teacher who sampled a number of inns and taverns on her journey from Boston to New York in 1704. Her journal challenges the image of the colonial tavern as an American agora in which freedom-loving citizens discoursed on the rights of man. In a Dedham tavern, seeking a guide for her journey, Knight asked the hostess to canvass the room. She received no response, as the men were "tyed by the Lipps" to their tankards. At a tavern in Rhode Island, she was kept up all night by two men arguing over the origin of the name Narragansett. (Her presence in an establishment serving drink caused no uproar: segregation by sex came only with Victorian manners and the temperance movement.)

The main attraction at any tavern, of course, was the refreshment. And here the native genius showed itself in full splendor. Every drink invited a dozen variations, every punch begged for an extra exotic ingredient to be thrown in. By temperament, Americans were never content to let well enough alone. In 1753, Isaac Acrelius, a pastor from Sweden, compiled a list of the drinks he encountered on a tour through the Delaware Valley. All but three of the forty-eight were alcoholic, beginning with "French wine" and proceeding through four kinds of cider and nearly twenty rum drinks (including punch, sling, and grog) to sangaree, syllabub, and mead. American beer he pronounced "brown, thick, and unpalatable."

Most of these drinks have gone the way of the pewter mug and the powdered wig. Cider royal, according to Acrelius, came in two versions. In the first, brandy was added to a barrel of cider along with several pounds of Muscovado (i.e., cane) sugar, which boosted the alcohol content and added flavor. If the ingredients were left to sit for a year, or sent on a sea voyage, the result was called apple wine. The second version of cider royal called for equal parts of cider and mead to be fermented together.

Syllabub, now a kind of dessert, loomed large in colonial drinking. A nineteenth-century article on the colonial tavern gives two recipes. The first: "Fill your syllabub pot with cider, and a good store of sugar; put in as much thick cream by two or three spoonfulls at a time, as hard as you can, as though you milk it, then stir it together exceedingly softly over and about and let it stand two hours at least." The second: "Take the juice and grated outer skin of a large lemon, four glasses of cider, ¼ pound sifted sugar, mix, let stand some hours, then whip it and add a pint of thick cream and the whites of two eggs cut to a froth." In her *American Cookery* (1796), Amelia Simmons takes a no-nonsense approach: "Sweeten a quart of cider with double refined sugar, grate nutmeg into it, then milk your cow into your liquor." The nineteenth century would have been scandalized to see the word "liquor" in a work meant for the family kitchen, but in colonial America, punches and syllabubs were simply part of the cuisine.

Many tavern menus offered sangaree. A corruption of the Spanish *sangría*, it was made by diluting red wine with water and lemon juice, then adding grated nutmeg and sometimes sugar. Sack-posset, a favorite at weddings and feasts, was ale and sherry thickened with eggs and cream, then seasoned with nutmeg, mace, and sugar, and boiled for two hours over a fire. Negus, named after a British colonel (d. 1732), was port or claret heated, sweetened with sugar, and flavored with lemon and grated nutmeg.

Not every tavern served all forty-eight of the drinks on Acrelius's roster, but most had a beverage menu of baroque complexity when compared with the shot-and-a-beer joint of modern times. A typical bill of fare, from a New York tavern in 1790, offered "good madeira wine" by the pint, other foreign wines, "fruit punch of good spirits and loaf sugar" in quart bowls, mulled cider, "egg or other sling, with a gill of West India rum in it and loaf sugar," West India rum, cherry rum, gin, brandy, cider royal, metheglin, "good double beer," and "good cyder." Gin, it should be noted, is but one of many offerings. In America it never attained anything like the popularity it enjoyed in England, where it was the universal tipple of the urban poor.

Nor did Acrelius exhaust the rum repertoire, even with twenty drinks. The plain man's approach was to mix his rum with a little water. Half and half made a sling. One part rum and three parts water was grog. Calibogus, or bogus, was cold rum and beer, unsweetened. Rum and cherry juice made cherry bounce. Bombo or bumbo was rum, sugar, water, and nutmeg; without the nutmeg, it became mimbo. Rum mixed with molasses was "black-strap," and country stores served it out of the barrel, which had a dried salted cod dangling alongside it, a free snack that usually encouraged extra orders, like the salted peanuts and potato chips that appear on most American bars as soon as the customer orders a beer.

Festive occasions inspired more fanciful rum drinks. Flip, which appeared around 1690, was beer sweetened with sugar, molasses, or dried pumpkin and strengthened with rum. A red-hot iron was thrust into the mixture, causing it to foam and take on a burnt, bitter flavor. The iron was known as a hottle, a flip dog, or a loggerhead, and its convenience as a weapon lies behind the expression "to be at logger-heads."

Recipes for flip varied, but the following, from Abbott's Tavern in Massachusetts, is typical:

> Keep grated ginger and nutmeg with a fine dried lemon peel rubbed together in a mortar. To make a quart of flip: put the ale on the fire to warm, and beat up three or four eggs with four ounces of moist sugar, a teaspoon of grated nutmeg or ginger, and a quartern of good old rum or brandy. When the ale is near to boil, put it into one pitcher, and the rum and eggs, etc., into another: turn it from one pitcher into another till it is as smooth as cream. To heat, plunge in the red-hot loggerhead or poker. This quantity is styled one yard of flannel.

The pride of most taverns, and a centerpiece of any festive occasion, was rum punch, flavored with shrub, lemon, or orange juice. Well into the nineteenth century, punch dominated whenever liquors were mixed. The most famous was Fish House Punch, the official drink of an eccentric social club—the peculiarly named State in Schuylkill— founded near Philadelphia in 1732 and still in existence. Its thirty members would periodically head out to the club's headquarters, a wooden castle on the Schuylkill River known as the Fish House, where they would don white aprons, fry perch on outdoor barbecue grills, and drink punch.

Legend credits a Captain Samuel Morris with inventing the punch, although one "governor" of the State in Schuylkill who looked into the matter decided that the ancient recipe came straight from a seventeenth-century punch favored by the Farmers' Club in London. Recipes for Fish House Punch abound, nearly all of them spurious. Dr. William Camac, governor of the State in Schuylkill, recorded the official one in 1873. It calls for one quart each of lemon juice and brandy, two quarts of rum, five pounds of sugar, and nine pounds of water and ice (four and a half quarts). It's a simple, even banal punch, and how it developed such a mystique remains unclear.

The American flair for improvisation and uninhibited mixing appeared early on, but the historian searches in vain for a proto-martini, or an Ur-Manhattan. Most drinks were hot, a legacy of the British drink culture, in which the first duty of an alcoholic beverage was to ward off the chill and damp. The colonists, as though unaware of America's blazing-hot summers, continued to favor drinks designed to stoke the internal stove. Ice, of course, was a luxury. But prevailing notions of physiology would have promoted the consumption of hot drinks in any case, and in any weather. Sweat drew heat from the body, and as a result, wrote one early chronicler, "the inner parts are left cold and faint."

No, the great ice age of drink lay in the future. The early Americans could do no more than clear the ground, then plant the seeds that would take root and yield a harvest for future generations. Their lasting contribution is the spirit of experiment and improvisation in matters of drink, still the great divide between the new and old worlds when it comes to mixing a cocktail. By breaking with tradition, and throwing off the dead hand of the past, they set the stage for the cocktail's triumph.

FIRST STIRRINGS

3

The cordial drop, the morning dram, I sing,
The mid-day toddy, and the evening sling.

—The Massachusetts Spy, *July 16, 1806*

As America picked up and headed west, it left rum behind and perfected the art of whiskey-making. That marks a giant step in the cocktail's evolution, for it was whiskey that predominated in the first recognizably modern mixed drinks. Whiskey was not entirely unknown to the colonists. At Jamestown in the early years of the seventeenth century, Captain George Thorpe distilled liquor from maize and dashed off a letter to London, exclaiming: "I have found a way to make so good a drink of Indian corn as I protest I have divers times refused to drink good strong English beer and chosen to drink that." When Governor Alexander Spotswood of Virginia led his "Knights of the Golden Horseshoe" across the Blue Ridge Mountains in 1716, hoping to find the Indian Ocean on the other side, his provisions included not only red and white wine from

Virginia, brandy, shrub, rum, champagne, canary, punch, water, and cider but also an unspecified quantity of "Irish usquebaugh"—that is, whiskey.

But virtually no whiskey was distilled before the Revolution. Isaac Acrelius, writing in the 1750s, reported that it was drunk "far up in the interior of the country, where rum is very dear on account of the transportation." Elsewhere, hard-to-grow grain made whiskey prohibitively expensive in comparison with rum. During the Revolutionary War, however, when neither rum nor molasses could be imported from the British West Indies, demand for spirits leapt, as thousands of men enlisted as soldiers. Suddenly, it became immensely profitable to distill rye and even wheat into whiskey, and the Scotch-Irish who had begun pouring into America in the 1730s had the know-how. The entrepreneurial response to this situation was so enthusiastic that it threatened the bread supply.

After the war was won, the pioneers who pushed across western Maryland and Pennsylvania soon found that it was cost-effective to distill rye into whiskey and ship it back in barrels. A pack horse could carry only four bushels of grain; but it could carry the equivalent of twenty-four bushels distilled into two kegs of whiskey. The process was simple enough. First, the grain was cooked in water to soften up the starch. This "mash" was then allowed to rest while the starch converted into sugar, which then underwent several days of fermentation after being exposed to yeast. In a pot still, the fermented slop was heated, causing a heady, alcoholic vapor to rise through a column and descend through a water-cooled tube. The change in temperature caused the vapor to condense, yielding precious raw whiskey, drop by drop. Soon there were five thousand log stillhouses in the frontier counties of Fayette, Allegheny, Westmoreland, and Washington, turning out the dry, piquant whiskey that would make the name Monongahela a byword for quality.

By 1788, a traveler reporting to the *Philadelphia Museum*, a newspaper, stated that "in the neighborhood of Pittsburgh almost every other farm has a stillhouse on it. . . . All the rye in those parts is distilled into whiskey, and wheat is often given in exchange for it. Plantations are often bought and sold for a certain number of barrels of whiskey. Indeed, whiskey in different quantities, like Montero's cap in *Tristram Shandy*, is the wager, the gift, and in some instances, the oath of three fourths of the inhabitants of our western counties." The whiskey habit, he noted, had spread to the German farmers of Lancaster and Berks counties, who poured the liquor over cucumbers at breakfast. The traveler may have been confused. François André Michaux, a Frenchman who toured the western frontier in 1805, reported that inhabitants of the hinterlands soaked the green cones of the so-called cucumber tree (actually a kind of magnolia) in whiskey to create a bitters that was thought to ward off fever.

Either way, whiskey had quickly become integrated into the fabric of daily life. George Washington himself went into the whiskey business. His last estate manager at Mount Vernon was a Scot named James Anderson, who persuaded Washington to turn over one of his unprofitable small farms to raising rye for whiskey. Soon Washington had a thriving operation that turned a profit of £83 in 1798, producing not only whiskey but apple, peach, and persimmon brandy. Jefferson, too, had a rye distillery.

It is ironic, then, that the distillation of whiskey should have led to the first test of federal power. In 1794, the farmers of Pennsylvania refused to pay excise tax on their whiskey, and Washington sent in the troops. Round one to the government.

But the disgruntled farmers of the Whiskey Rebellion simply pushed west into Kentucky, and there, where corn grew abundantly, they invented America's most enduring gift to the world of spirits: bourbon whiskey.

Just who can lay claim to the invention of bourbon remains unclear. George Thorpe, back in Jamestown in the early seventeenth century, distilled a kind of whiskey from corn, which entitles him to a footnote in bourbon history. But modern bourbon is a far different product, distilled from corn and a small percentage of rye or wheat and aged in charred new oak barrels. The result is a plump, fruity, russet-colored whiskey. Its evolution is obscure, shrouded as it is in myth, self-interested claims, and folk history.

We know that distilling was taking place on the western frontier even before the Whiskey Rebellion. Corn and rye were grown in Kentucky during the Revolution, and scattered references suggest that stills were operating in the 1770s and 1780s. In 1789, George Thatcher, a Massachusetts congressman, ridiculed the "new-fangled distillates produced in other states," made from such raw ingredients as rye, apples, and peaches.

In 1776, Elijah Pepper settled near Lexington, Kentucky, and he reportedly set up a still circa 1780. The family firm, which flourished under Elijah's grandson James E. Pepper, produced a whiskey called Old 1776, whose slogan, "Born with the Republic," may have been an exaggeration, but only a slight one. Whether Elijah Pepper was producing genuine bourbon as early as 1780 seems doubtful. Another perennial candidate in the bourbon sweepstakes is Evan Williams, officially registered as the first man to open a distillery in Kentucky, in 1783.

Traditionally, credit for inventing Kentucky bourbon has gone to the Reverend Elijah Craig, who supposedly turned out the first true bourbon in 1789 at Georgetown in Scott County. Gerald Carson, in his *Social History of Bourbon,* calls the Craig claim history, if history is defined as "fiction agreed upon." Henry G. Crowgey, in his scholarly *Kentucky Bourbon,* writes reasonably that "what actually happened was that a people moved in who regarded liquor as a necessity of life." And in the same mysterious way that the folk music of Ireland evolved into the bluegrass music of the Appalachians, its whiskey became bourbon.

Initially, the "new-fangled distillate" was known simply as whiskey, but gradually it became obvious that Kentucky was turning out a superior product—full-bodied, mellow, and smooth. By the early nineteenth century, "Kentucky whiskey" and "Western whiskey" were recognized trade terms, and the term "Bourbon whiskey" appears in 1821. But bourbon might simply have indicated the place of origin rather than a style: the original Bourbon County embraced all or part of modern Kentucky's thirty-four counties, so "bourbon whiskey" and "Kentucky whiskey" were more or less synonymous. As the century wore on, the term "Old Bourbon" came into use. Today, straight bourbon whiskey refers to a spirit made from a mash of no less than 51 percent corn and aged in charred new white oak barrels for at least two years. (If the grain content is 51 percent rye, the result is rye whiskey, while Scotch is made from barley and can be aged in new or old casks, charred or uncharred.)

But was the whiskey really bourbon? Unlike true bourbon, the early-nineteenth-century product was colorless, and the charring of casks (probably an effort to remove unwanted flavors from old casks that had been used for nonwhiskey purposes, or to burn off the splinters and blisters of new casks) seems to have developed much later in the century.

Whatever its origins, bourbon eventually produced one of the earliest and greatest of American cocktails: the mint julep. The word comes from the Arabic *julab,* or rose water, and can be found in Milton, but in its modern meaning it first appears in 1787. A Virginian of the lower or middle class, runs this early citation, "rises in the morning, about 6 o'clock. He then drinks a julap, made of rum, water, and sugar, but very strong." Clearly, this is not the bourbon-and-mint julep we know today, but a precursor. The first reference to mint comes in 1803, when an English traveler, John Davis, who was employed as a tutor on a Virginia plantation, explained that a julep was "a dram of spirituous liquor that has mint in it, taken by Virginians of a morning." Evidently, news of the julep was slow to travel northward, since Webster's 1806 dictionary defines it as "a kind of liquid medicine."

Frederick Marryat, an English naval officer who toured the United States in the 1830s, was also fascinated by the julep, and he noted the recipe:

> Put into a tumbler about a dozen tender shoots of mint, upon them put a spoonful of white sugar, and equal proportions of peach and common brandy, so as to fill up one third, or perhaps a little less. Then take rasped or pounded ice, and fill up the tumbler. Epicures rub the lip of the tumbler with a piece of fresh pineapple, and the tumbler itself is very often encrusted outside with stalactites of ice. As the ice melts, you drink.

The lavish use of ice marks the julep as an aristocratic drink. Before commercial ice harvesting began in the mid-nineteenth century, only substantial estates or hotels maintained icehouses.

The julep appears to have been a popular everyday drink, the Coca-Cola of its time. Basil Hall, yet another traveling Englishman, reported that in the course of a seventeen-hour journey in Virginia in the late 1820s, his stagecoach stopped at ten different public houses. At each stop, his companions alighted to drink a mint julep. Hall expressed amazement that, except for the slight slurring of the speech and an increasing earnestness in their discussions, his fellow journeyers seemed none the worse for wear at the end of the trip.

In his modern treatise on the mint julep, Richard Barksdale Harwell wrote that "the mint julep originated in the northern Virginia tidewater, spread soon to Maryland, and eventually all along the seaboard and even to transmontane Kentucky." At first, he says, it was made with the local whiskey—rye. The 1787 citation mentioned above indicates that rum was used as well. By the 1830s, the julep more or less corresponded to Marryat's recipe. The well-to-do used brandy, while others used whiskey. After the Civil War, with the South impoverished, brandy disappeared entirely, and the bourbon mint julep became universal.

Harwell is not exactly an unprejudiced witness. His pamphlet, published by the University Press of Virginia, is dedicated to the proposition that the julep can only be Virginian—nay, that bourbon itself is Virginian, since what is now Kentucky formed part of Virginia until 1792. That includes Bourbon County. Virginia, as a matter of fact, continues to produce bourbon today—Virginia Gentleman, made by the state's only distillery, Smith Bowman.

In pressing Virginia's claims, Harwell keeps alive a controversy that has been raging for decades. In truth, the wrangling is tedious, carried on in ponderously "humorous" newspaper editorials. On occasion, a Virginia paper will decide to antagonize Kentucky by asserting once more that bourbon, and therefore the julep, originated in the Old Dominion State. Usually this occurs around Kentucky Derby time, for maximum impact. The joke lies in Kentucky's being seen as a kind of shabby, down-market version of Virginia. Kentucky, for its part, considers Virginia to be snooty and stuck-up. "We have lived to see the Emperor of Japan confess that he is not a god," wrote the *Louisville Courier-Journal* in a 1946 julep-inspired tirade, "but we do not expect to live to hear a Virginian say Virginians are no better than other people."

If the mark of a great cocktail is the number of arguments it can provoke and the number of unbreakable rules it generates, the mint julep may be America's preeminent classic, edging out the martini in a photo finish. When weary of the Virginia-Kentucky debate, julep fanciers can filibuster for days on the mint issue: whether 'tis nobler to bruise or crush. (In fact, it doesn't matter very much.) When tired of bickering over mint leaves, julep pedants can tackle another co-nundrum: Should it be sipped from the glass or through a straw? This point of contention, perpetually on the simmer, boiled over on a slow news day, when the *Courier-Journal* decided to lay down the law: Straws are mandatory, to keep the face out of the mint shrubbery. Kentucky has only to speak, and Virginia becomes irate. The *Richmond Times-Dispatch* shot back that straws are fit only for lemonade and sarsaparilla, adding for good measure: "juleps aren't worth drink-ing, when consumed in the Kentucky manner." Less crucial but nonetheless stimulating points of dispute concern ice (cubes, shaved ice, or fine powder?), sugar (syrup or granulated?), drinking vessel (glass or silver?), type of bourbon (straight or blend?), and so on, ad infinitum.

If there can be any such thing as the official julep recipe, the honors must go to the statesman Henry Clay. By birth a Virginian, he represented Kentucky for more than fifty years in the House and Senate, and he mixed his juleps thusly:

Mint leaves, fresh and tender, should be pressed against a coin-silver goblet and the back of a silver spoon. Only bruise the leaves gently and then remove from the goblet. Half fill with cracked ice. Mellow Bourbon is poured from the jigger and allowed to slide slowly through the cracked ice. In another receptacle, granulated sugar is slowly mixed into chilled limestone water [water that has flowed through limestone and is therefore hard] then poured on top of the ice. While beads of moisture gather on the burnished exterior of the goblet, garnish the frosted brim with the choicest sprig of mint. Then sip.

Clay's julep recipe is heartfelt, even noble. Rarely does a great statesman render homage to a great cocktail. But America's most significant julep was drunk far from Bourbon County. The place: Baltimore. The year: 1842. The tipplers: Charles Dickens and Washington Irving. On his first tour of America, Dickens recalled:

Some unknown admirer of his books and mine sent to the hotel a most enormous mint julep, wreathed in flowers. We sat, one on either side of it, with great solemnity (it filled a respectably-sized round table) but the solemnity was of very short duration. It was quite an enchanted julep, and carried us among innumerable people and places that we both knew. The julep held out far into the night, and my memory never saw him afterwards otherwise than as bending over it, with his straw, with an attempted air of gravity (after some anecdote involving some wonderfully droll and delicate observation of character), and then as his eye caught mine, melting into that captivating laugh of his, which was the brightest and best that I have ever heard.

The julep, alas, scarcely exists today except as a rather strained evocation of the Old South. Thousands are served each Memorial Day in Louisville at the Kentucky Derby, but the gesture is purely nostalgic. As a living part of the culture, the julep has gone the way of the plantation house and hoop skirts. The drink reached its nadir in the 1950s, when a shortcut julep reared its head: a cold shot of bourbon stirred with a stick of green peppermint candy. This quickie version of the old cocktail underscored, in the crudest possible way, the central weakness of the julep: it was always a slow, complicated drink, requiring a servant class to make it. Ordering it is tantamount to saying, "Peel me a grape." Today, it is little more than a caricature of Southern leisure. R.I.P.

The mixing of whiskey, bitters, and sugar marks a turning point, as decisive for American drinking habits as the discovery of three-point perspective was for Renaissance painting. It is the beginning of the cocktail in a recognizably modern form. The prevailing virtues of warmth and nourishment were giving way to refreshment and stimulation; the communal atmosphere of the tavern and hostelry to the less settled patterns of the barroom; and the punch bowl to the individual drink, often idiosyncratic, crafted individually for each customer.

The radical changes in American tastes can be traced in the remarkable explosion of drink terms in the early nineteenth century. The most important is the appearance of the word "cocktail" itself. On May 13, 1806, subscribers to *The Balance and Columbian Repository* were treated to a lively exchange on the letters page. A week earlier, the Hudson, New York, paper had made passing reference to an odd word, which provoked an inquiry from a puzzled reader:

> Sir, I observe in your paper of the 6th inst., in the account of a democratic candidate for a seat in the Legislature, marked under the head of Loss, 25 do., "cocktail." Will you be so obliging as to

inform me what is meant by this species of refreshment? . . . I have heard of a "jorum," of "phlegm cutter" and "fog driver," of "wetting the whistle" and "moistening the clay," of a "fillip," a "spur in the head," "quenching a spark in the throat," of "flip," etc., but never in my life, though I have lived a good many years, did I hear of cocktail before. Is it peculiar to a part of this country? Or is it a late invention? Is the name expressive of the effect which the drink has on a particular part of the body? Or does it signify that the Democrats who make the potion are turned topsy turvy, and have their heads where their tails are?

The editor's answer:

Cocktail is a stimulating liquor, composed of spirits of any kind, sugar, water, and bitters—it is vulgarly called bittered sling and is supposed to be an excellent engineering potion, inasmuch as it renders the heart stout and bold, at the same time that it fuddles the head. It is said also, to be of great use to a Democratic candidate: because, a person having swallowed a glass of it, is ready to swallow anything else.

This is the first known reference to the cocktail in its present meaning, although the thing itself predated the word. Charles William Janson, an Englishman who toured the United States between 1793 and 1806, told his readers that "the first craving of an American in the morning, is for ardent spirits, mixed with sugar, mint, or some other hot herb, and which are called slings." If his "hot herb" means bitters—an alcoholic infusion of bitter herbs, leaves, or roots that act as a stimulant to the palate—then he was describing the same "bittered sling" referred to by the editor of the *Balance*.

Early observers seem to agree that the key ingredient defining a cocktail was bitters. When Edward Henry Durrell, visiting New Orleans in the 1840s, expressed puzzlement at the term "brandy cocktail," an obliging native gave him a quick tutorial: "Now the difference between a brandy cocktail and a brandy toddy is this: a brandy toddy is made by adding together a little water, a little sugar, and a great deal of brandy—mix well and drink. A brandy cocktail is composed of the same ingredients, with the addition of a shade of Stoughton's bitters; so that the bitters draw the line of demarcation."

The word "cocktail" itself remains one of the most elusive in the language. Many writers on drink have accepted the legend of Betsy Flanagan, the widow of a Revolutionary War soldier who supposedly kept a Westchester tavern frequented by French soldiers (the town is given as Four Corners or Elmsford). One day in 1779, the story goes, she plucked a few feathers from the roosters kept by a neighbor who happened to be a Tory. In a celebratory toast, her customers cried out, "Vive le cocktail!"

Let us examine this thoroughly spurious anecdote, for it bears many of the distinctive features of the fake explanations that abound in the literature on drink. First, like a bad alibi, it is at once too vague and too specific. The idea that the whim of a moment—placing a cock's "tail" in a glass on a particular evening—would generate a new word that passed forever into the American vocabulary strains credulity. Furthermore, as we have seen, the word does not appear in print until 1806. In any case, the mixed English and French of "Vive le cocktail!" is ludicrous.

The Flanagan story is a striking example of what might be called barroom etymology, a pseudodiscipline that bears the same relation to real etymology that barroom conversation does to the philosophy of Hegel. It rests on the wobbly premise that each and every cocktail was invented on a specific occasion by a particular bartender, who looked upon his new drink, cried Eureka! and endowed it with a fanciful name. Because this notion has a grip on the popular mind, nearly every drink comes fitted out with a preposterous origin story, concocted according to the following rules: Spin a yarn, embellish it, throw in a few colorful details for that authentic feel (while keeping the main points a little vague). Buff and polish in the retelling. After three repetitions, present as historical fact.

Betsy Flanagan first surfaces in a work of fiction: James Fenimore Cooper's *The Spy*, published in 1821 but set in the 1780s. Often described as the first novel to use purely American themes, it presents Betty Flanagan as a military widow running a hotel in Four Corners. Although bibulous and slatternly, she has a stout patriot's heart. In addition, "Betty had the merit of being the inventor of that beverage which is so well-known, at the present hour, to all the patriots who make a winter's march between the commercial and political capitals of this great state, and which is distinguished by the name of 'cocktail.' " Cooper remains tantalizingly silent on the sort of drinks his character serves, but he does mention that from her Virginia customers, Betty picked up the habit of using mint.

All this is interesting, but is it history? We know that Cooper relied on the oral testimony of Revolutionary War veterans in assembling material for *The Spy*, most of whose characters and locations are rooted in historical fact. It is therefore possible that an old soldier credited Flanagan with inventing the cocktail, but even that much is pure speculation.

Frustration in the search for the word's origin has driven lexicographers to make some wild leaps. Richard Manning Chipman, who assisted Bartlett in compiling his famous 1877 *Dictionary of Americanisms*, speculated in his notebooks that "this term seems to have been suggested by the shape which froth, as of a glass of porter, etc., assumed when it flows over the side of the tumbler, etc., containing the liquid effervescing." In other words, the foam looked like the docked tail of a dray horse, known as a cocktail.

In a similarly fanciful vein, the *New York World* in 1891 said that the word was of Aztec origin, claiming that the cocktail was invented by "a Toltec noble" who ordered his daughter, Xochitl, to bring a sample to the king. "Xochitl," of course, became "cocktail." More recently, but no less feebly, a linguist has suggested that the word comes from the West African *kaketal,* or scorpion, which, like a well-prepared martini, has a sting.

We arrive on more plausible ground with the hypothesis that "cocktail" derives from the French *coquetel,* a term for mixed drink current in Bordeaux and introduced to America by French soldiers fighting in the Revolution. The French argument has the merit of taking as its protagonist a bona fide historical figure, Antoine Peychaud, a New Orleans apothecary known for the brandy and bitters he served in egg cups known as "coquetiers." (Peychaud's bitters, still made today by the Sazerac Co. of New Orleans, are an essential ingredient in the Sazerac cocktail.) When pronounced by English speakers, "coquetier" became "cocktay," and thence it was but a short jump to "cocktail."

But the word may just as likely be of English origin. "Cock ale" was ale in which a pulverized and spiced red cock had been steeped for a week or so. The recipe deserves to be recorded:

> Take ten gallons of ale and a large cock, the older the better; parboil the cock, flay him, and stamp him in a stone mortar till his bones are broken (you must craw and gut him when you flay him), then put the cock into two quarts of sack, and put it to three pounds of raisins of the sun stoned, some blades of mace and a few cloves;

> put all these into a canvas bag, and a little before you find the ale
> has done working, put the ale and bag together into a vessel; in a
> week or nine days bottle it up, fill the bottles but just above the
> neck, and give it the same time to ripen as other ale.

All very interesting, but cock ale and cocktail show no meaningful similarities, unlike Peychaud's egg-cup concoctions.

A more persuasive—or at least ingenious—case for the English origin of the word appears in H. L. Mencken's *The American Language*. According to a Pennsylvania correspondent, "In many English taverns the last of the liquor drawn from barrels of ardent spirits, otherwise the cock-tailings, were thrown together in a common receptacle. This mixture was sold to topers at a reduced price, so naturally they would call for *cocktails*." Mencken explains that "cock" referred to a valve or spigot, and "tailings" to dregs or leavings.

Enough. Whatever its origins, the word quickly passed into general usage. Washington Irving, in 1809, refers to "cock-tail, stone-fence, and sherry-cobbler" as "recondite beverages," but within a few years the cocktail was recondite no more. The mixed drink became universal throughout the land.

It must have tasted good—"Makes a feller wish he had a throat a mile long and a palate at every inch of it," one early enthusiast reported—because between the 1790s and 1830, Americans were consuming spirituous liquors at triple today's rate. No one can quite explain why, although commonsense theories abound. Price was certainly no deterrent. Whiskey, virtually untaxed, sold for as little as twenty-five cents a gallon. Drink may have provided relief from a monotonous diet heavy on salted meats. Constant indigestion, the natural consequence of a leaden, fatty cuisine, created a land-office business for any mixture that could penetrate grease and get the gastric juices flowing. Drink offered an escape from hard and unremitting labor. And, just as in colonial days, liquor was thought to build strength and promote health. At least one nineteenth-century insurance company imposed a surcharge on abstainers, regarded as weak and weedy, and unquestionably a bad health risk.

The morning eye-opener seemed no more remarkable to Americans of the time than a mouthwash rinse does today. The "anti-fogmatic," taken as directed ("in exact proportion to the thickness of the fog," according to the *Massachusetts Spy* in 1789), was thought to ward off the fever and ague that a fog in the throat could cause. In 1821, the Lancaster, Pennsylvania, *Journal* provided a humorous taxonomy of the anti-fogmatic, dividing it into four genuses: "gum tickler" ("warms the gums, and removes bad taste from the mouth after sleeping"), "phlegm cutter," "gall breaker," and "clear comforter." Twenty species were enumerated as well.

Visitors to the United States almost uniformly depicted *Homo americanus* with a plug of tobacco in his cheek and whiskey on his breath, whatever the hour. By 1822, an anonymous writer was defining a simple Kentucky breakfast as "three cocktails and a chaw of terbacker." This may not have been fanciful. A tavern bill from 1812 shows that one gentleman guest consumed three mint slings before breakfast—not to mention nine tumblers of grog before dinner, three glasses of wine and bitters with dinner, and, just to put a smooth gloss on the meal, two "ticklers" of French brandy afterward.

Perhaps what Frederick Marryat called "the pleasantness, amenity, and variety of the potations" in America had something to do with the rise in consumption, although here the historian sees through a shot glass, darkly. The bittered sling seems to have been universal, as well as its close cousin, the mint julep. Punches and cobblers—wine or spirit, sugar, and a festive garnish of fruits—are frequently cited.

Likewise the Stone Fence, also known as the Stone Wall, a mixture of brandy and cider. But recipes are rarely to be found. Charles Dickens, on his 1842 tour of the United States, encountered something called the Timber Doodle in Boston. Alas, he failed to record the ingredients.

The lack of evidence is frustrating, because it is precisely at this period that ice enters the picture, a landmark step in the evolution of the cocktail. Ice was not unknown, of course, even to the colonists. Well-to-do farmers in the Northeast maintained pondside icehouses, and hotels depended on ice deliveries for food preservation. But ice remained a luxury for most citizens. When available, it went to produce ice cream. "Ice was jewelry," Mark Twain wrote. "Only the rich could wear it."

But after the 1830s, with the invention of the ice plow, ice harvesting became a commercial proposition. Production soared, and the price dropped—enough, apparently, to influence the preparation of mixed drinks. In 1835, a citation appears for the hailstorm (or hailstone)—ardent spirit with small lumps of ice. The snowstorm, ingredients unknown, also suggests cold.

Exactly when and where ice first hit glass is impossible to say, for the chilling of the cocktail had already taken place by the time Jerry Thomas published his path-breaking *Bar-tender's Guide* in 1862. His book and its subsequent imitators called for ice in all forms: shaved, broken, and cracked, and served in lumps both large and small. The bartender or his assistants worked with ice pick, shaver, and mallet on a large cake, sometimes encased in a canvas money sack for convenience. In proper establishments, the final product was washed before being deposited in the patron's glass with an ice scoop or a pair of tongs.

Gradually, ice came to be regarded, not as a flashy option, but as an essential cocktail ingredient. In 1889, the English lexicographer John S. Farmer defined the cocktail as

> a wineglassful of brandy, whiskey, gin, or other spirit, to which is added a teaspoonful of bitters (mostly Angostura); this, with a pinch of sugar and crushed ice, according to taste, is then whisked briskly round, until the mixture, sparkling and foaming, nearly overruns the glass in which it is made. It should be served "hot," as the Yankees say, i.e., while still frothing and foaming.

As Farmer's exuberance suggests, the introduction of ice had the kind of transformative effect on cocktails that electric lighting did on cities. The bittered sling took on an entirely different character when mixed up with crushed ice. It became fresher, more exciting, racy. A new sense of energy emanated from the cocktail, as the limitless possibilities of the form begin to open up. As America became an urban, industrial country, the pace of invention accelerated, and the cocktail entered its era of greatness.

SWINGING DOORS

4

I doted on the cool,
refreshing scent of a good saloon
on a hot summer day.

–H. L. Mencken, Happy Days (1940)

The saloon must go.

–Motto of the Anti-Saloon League

The cocktail, a gifted but struggling amateur in the early years of the Republic, comes into its own with the rise of the saloon in the nineteenth century. Like most of our national institutions, the saloon evolved gradually, nourished by English roots yet reaching instinctively toward a purely American form. Over time, the colonial tavern, offering food, drink, and accommodations, found some of its functions taken over by more specialized operations: the hotel, the restaurant, and the saloon, a temple of drink presided over by a kind of democratic high priest, the bartender.

The word "saloon" conjures up a picture of swinging doors, player pianos, and six-shooters, but its spirit and its origins are urban. Long before rude entrepreneurs were pitching canvas tents and dispensing whiskey from the barrel on the mining frontier, the saloon was a glittering palace on the city streets, a sparkling wonderland of polished brass, mirrors, and cut crystal. By the time Prohibition rolled around, the saloon would be synonymous with drinking at its worst: a reeking dive dispensing rotgut at a few cents a shot, tempting the workingman into throwing away his meager wages, starting out the nation's youth on the fast track to hell. But it didn't start out that way.

On a summer day in 1839, an Austrian traveler named Francis Grund decided to escape the sweltering heat of New York by heading out to the north shore of Staten Island and a hotel known as the Pavilion. There he found the American saloon at its finest. Wines and spirits from all over the world were arrayed behind the bar, set off by carefully arranged piles of lemons and oranges. Because of the heat, the Pavilion was doing a land-office business in mint juleps. The newcomer spied "a huge mass of ice and a forest of mint, together with two large bottles of French and peach brandy."

Not many Americans had seen anything quite so impressive, but as the century wore on, fancy saloons appeared in every American city. They were intended to dazzle and overwhelm, in the Victorian manner, with a heavy-gun, all-out decorative onslaught. Woodwork was massive and heavy, ceilings high, glassware ornate. "I have visited in my day the barrooms of all civilized countries," Mencken wrote in the 1940s, "but none that I ever saw came within miles of a high-toned American saloon of the Golden Age. Today the influence of the cocktail lounge has brought in blue glass, chrome fixtures and bars of puny and pale woods, but in the time I speak of, saloon architects stuck to mirrors as God first made them, to honest brass, and to noble and imperishable mahogany."

Even the lesser fry made some gesture, however feeble, toward monumental effect. In the same way that every American town billed itself as the fastest-growing burg in the U.S., all saloons claimed to have a bar of epic proportions. In the West, land of the tall tale and the big boast, rare was the establishment that did not advertise its "mile-long bar," which, although longer than the mile-long hot dog, generally measured 100 feet or so. In Portland, Oregon, however, thirsty loggers could belly up to 684 feet of solid mahogany at Erickson's on Burnside Street.

The fanciest bars were found in the grand hotels, which operated as semipublic institutions. Nonguests felt free to stroll into a fine hotel lobby, settle down in a comfortable chair, and read a newspaper—or even write a letter or two on the house stationery. The bars and restaurants of the top hotels served as rallying points for captains of industry, brokers, assorted moneymen, journalists, and political heavyweights. The "Amen Corner," two pairs of red plush settees just outside the bar of the Fifth Avenue Hotel in New York, saw more high-level political dealing than any place outside the halls of Congress. The Republican State Committee maintained its headquarters there for years, and when the hotel closed its doors, in 1908, the settees were formally donated to the Museum of the City of New York and the New-York Historical Society.

The most celebrated of the swank bars could be found at New York's Hoffman House, which opened in the fall of 1864. Located at Twenty-fifth Street and Broadway, the hotel had a barroom that ran a full seventy-five feet along Twenty-fourth Street. Behind its heavy carved mahogany bar, seventeen bartenders worked, their images reflected in wall mirrors said to be the largest in America. The mirrors ran a poor second, however, to the beguiling *Nymphs and Satyr*, a large painting by Bouguereau purchased for $10,010 by the hotel's proprietor, Edward S. Stokes, fresh out of Sing Sing for the murder of

Jim Fisk, the Wall Street speculator. Florid, overblown, and frankly erotic, the painting simply overpowered the bar's other canvases, even the nude-intensive *Vision of Faust*.

It was the age of "more is more," and not only in decoration. America took an uncomplicated attitude toward wealth and display. When the rich ate, they didn't pick at a minimalist arrangement of steamed *haricots verts*. No, they gorged; they sat down to epic, heart-stopping meals that could make two-ton mahogany tables sag. The fat sizzled, the wine flowed in torrents, and entire animal populations suffered drastic decline. There was nothing furtive about any of this. The oxymoronic notion of intimate public space did not exist. Life outside the home was lived on a theatrical, heroic scale. It was an age of high living and free spending, of large men with large appetites. "Them was the days when everybody drank champagne," one Hoffman House bartender recalled wistfully, looking back from the Depression year of 1930.

For pure, gorgeous, unfettered display, for the sheer exuberance of wealth, the United States has never really matched its performance in the period between the Civil War and the First World War. In 1860, there were perhaps twenty millionaires in America; by 1880 there were a hundred, and that number would increase to more than four thousand in 1890 and forty thousand in 1916. Cheap labor and no income tax allowed the rich to live like kings, and their opulent style set the tone. Not many New York swells could afford to spend $100,000 on a dinner at Delmonico's, like Diamond Jim Brady, but they could and did stand rounds for the house and call out for quarts of champagne. The great saloons provided a glittering stage for the grand gesture.

The Hoffman House, a favorite with Democratic politicians, the Tammany machine, and the sporting element, prided itself on its fine wines and liquors. William F. Mulhall, who began tending bar at the hotel in 1882, recalled Rhine wine at eighteen dollars a bottle—the equivalent of two hundred dollars today. At one grand occasion, when one of the city's German societies held a banquet, one hundred fifty guests sat down with one bottle of Rhine wine each in front of them. Brandy, regarded as just a bit old-fashioned by the late nineteenth century, came in a little stone jug at fifty cents, although the bar kept a fifty-year-old Hennessy cognac, which it served at one dollar a drink. "That was the highest price ever known for a drink of liquor in America up to that time," wrote Mulhall, "and sometimes the check used to 'faze' the newcomer who called for 'the best.' "

The splurge drink was champagne, and it flowed through the cities of late-nineteenth-century America like a mighty, coursing river. Money and champagne always seek each other out. In the roaring eighties of the twentieth century, Dom Pérignon—"D.P." for short— became the Gatorade of the Wall Street warrior, the official beverage of the stock market Olympics. So, too, a hundred years ago, the booming market and an expanding industrial economy demanded champagne—and lots of it. Consumption was boosted by gregarious wine buyers, familiar figures in all the better saloons. A cross between a door-to-door salesman and a professional host, the wine buyer would treat lavishly with the champagne he represented, then move along to the next bar up the street. Ordering a quart bottle rather than a pint automatically identified the customer as a "sport," while the half-gallon magnum, according to an anonymous memoir, "was the special 'tour de force' of the high roller, the wine agent, and the spender."

For every Hoffman House, of course, there were innumerable humble corner saloons, with a long, scuffed wooden bar and sawdust on the floor. A voluptuous Venus hung on one wall, and John L. Sullivan, in fighting posture, on another. Behind the bar were humorous cards on the order of "If Drinking Interferes With Your Business, Cut Out Business."

"When you had visited one of the old-time saloons you had seen a thousand," wrote George Ade, the Indiana satirist, in his dry-eyed history of the pre-Prohibition bar.

> Very often it stood on a corner so as to have two street entrances and wave a gilded beer sign at pedestrians drifting along from any point of the compass. The entrance was through swinging doors which were shuttered so that anyone standing on the outside could not see what was happening on the inside. The windows were masked by grille work, potted ferns, one-sheet posters, and a fly-specked array of fancy-shaped bottles which were merely symbols and not merchandise.

Cocktails were for sissies. The drinks were whiskey, drunk straight, and beer. Branded whiskeys were for the select few. Most customers ordered rye or bourbon, distinguishable by the shapes of their bottles, which were filled from two-to-three-gallon jugs, which in turn were filled from barrels in the basement. The bartender placed a two-and-a-half-ounce glass on the bar, with water on the side. The customer poured his own drink. As for cocktails, "the plain sturdy bartender of our neighborhood was likely to come up with a mixture made by guess and by God," wrote a Cincinnatian recalling the 1880s saloon.

Out West, the setup could be even more primitive: a canvas tent and a few barrels dispensing "cowboy cocktails," or straight whiskey. But the iconic saloon of a thousand B Westerns should not be taken at face value. True, the earliest bars were as crude as their customers and their whiskey, which was prized for strength, not subtlety. The real stuff—and it could be alcohol revved up with red pepper and tobacco—was known as "40 rod" (said to be powerful enough to stun a man at that distance), "extract of scorpions," "chain lightning," "stagger juice," and "panther's breath." A shot of the right whiskey could "draw a blood blister on a rawhide boot." Sometimes it tasted like footwear; on the Klondike, gold miners added piquancy to their whiskey by throwing in old boots and unwashed foot rags during distillation.

But there's ample evidence that the Western saloon could be fancy enough for the most persnickety Eastern dude. San Francisco, of course, rivaled New Orleans and New York as a capital of food and drink. But even lesser towns could offer the visitor a topflight saloon with a thoroughly professional bartender in full command of the drink repertoire.

Corvelo, California, could not have been a sophisticated metropolis in 1873, but a visitor from *Harper's* magazine was handed the following gilt-edged "Toddy Time-Table" on entering the local saloon:

6 A.M.	Eye Opener	3 P.M.	Cobbler
7 "	Appetizer	4 "	Social Drink
8 "	Digester	5 "	Invigorator
9 "	Big Reposer	6 "	Solid Straight
10 "	Refresher	7 "	Chit-chat
11 "	Stimulant	8 "	Fancy Smile
12 M.	Ante-Lunch	9 "	Entire [sic] Act
1 P.M.	Settler	10 "	Sparkler
2 "	à la Smythe	11 "	Rouser
		12 P.M.	Night Cap

It is possible, of course, that the dedicated patrons of the saloon stuck to a shot of "tornado juice" throughout the busy day, but the schedule suggests a taste for finer things.

The most famous feature of the saloon was the free lunch. As nearly as anyone can tell, the institution began in New Orleans in the late 1830s at the Café des Réfugiés, where the management began offering a midday menu of soup, a piece of beef or ham with potatoes, meat pie, and oyster patties. Not surprisingly, business picked up. Soon the practice spread throughout the city, and beyond.

For decades afterward, a glass of beer served as a ticket to a side table loaded down with the fixings for a noontime repast. At the more expensive establishments, the food was good—so good that, according to one turn-of-the-century observer, "the profit is hard to understand. You pay 10 cents for a glass of beer and you tip the waiter 10 cents. For his 10 cents the waiter brings you a napkin, a 50-cent slice of roast beef, 25 cents worth of potatoes, 10 cents worth of beets, 5 cents worth of bread, and 10 cents worth of cheese." The lunch table at the old Waldorf in New York, offering canapés, anchovies, Virginia ham, and assorted cheeses and crudités, cost the hotel $75,000 a year.

But the more typical nickel-a-beer saloons offered a humble spread of ham, baked beans, pretzels, dried herring, pickles, head cheese, hot dogs, stews, chowders, and hot soups, all heavily salted to inspire another round of drinks. At some bars, patrons could expect nothing better than cheese, stale crackers, and onions. The proprietors regarded the free lunch as a necessary evil and did not spend a lot of time on the niceties. Nearly all commentators on the old saloon recall with a shudder of disgust the serving fork kept in a goblet of swampy-looking water. Bartenders had to keep a sharp eye out for "free-lunch fiends," who would sidle up to the lunch counter without buying a drink.

Many men retained a nostalgic view of the saloon during the arid years of Prohibition, a testing time that lasted from 1920 to 1934.

Selective memory smoothed over the rough spots and caused the more attractive features to shine with a double luster. The aroma of stale beer and sawdust was a heavenly scent for the American male, ripe with the promise of boon companionship and lively but undemanding conversation. In bygone days, when the workingman lived in a cramped, dismal tenement, and the middle-class home lacked the smorgasbord of technological delights that dazzle the present age, the corner bar beckoned seductively. All but the most abject bars offered at least the pretense of splendor and elegance. For an hour or two, the man of small means could live like a nabob, surrounded by cut glass and polished wood, waited on by a professional in starched linen.

But there was more to it than that. The saloon was a democratic arena in which a man could count on being taken at his own valuation, where his opinion counted for just as much as his drinking partner's. Freed from the demeaning hierarchies of the workplace, men could mingle and philosophize as equals. At home and at work, the average American man cut a less than heroic figure. The saloon offered escape, the opportunity to project a different, more dashing image before an uncritical audience. It might be said that only in the saloon could a man reach his full potential. There, in the midst of approving peers—the kind of fellows who could be counted on to laugh even when they'd heard the joke before—he could glance in the mirror and see reflected a masculine paragon: a wit, a bit of a rogue, and still, all things considered, surprisingly youthful. All this for the price of a beer.

THE ICEMAN COMETH

5

*Bartending is an old
and honorable trade.*

**–Patrick Gavin Duffy,
The Official Mixer's Manual (1934)**

When Francis Grund took in the scene at the Pavilion in 1839, he found himself fascinated by the frantic activity of the man behind the bar, "preparing ice-punch, mint-juleps, port and madeira *sangarie*, apple toddy, gin sling, etc., with a celerity of motion of which I had heretofore scarcely seen an example." Here was something strange and wonderful: a man whose sole occupation was to mix outlandish drinks. He was the bartender, equal parts chef, conjurer, and juggler, the unsung hero of the golden age of cocktails.

Where he came from, no one knows. The word "bartender" first appears in 1836, but the origins of the profession remain obscure and the early practitioners of the trade can be seen only by a fitful, flickering light—in the rare observation of a traveler or the brief descriptive passage of a novelist.

He was a commanding and rather aristocratic figure. Dressed in a sparkling white tunic, generally sporting a handlebar mustache with waxed ends, his cuffs kept free of the glasses by ornamental sleeve garters, he was sommelier, actor, and shaman, an adept in the arcana of the cocktail, a repository of sporting knowledge, and a master of the art of conversing without ever expressing an opinion.

Early observers marveled at the barman's flashy technique. In Hawthorne's *Blithedale Romance* (1852), the narrator chances to observe a master at work:

> With a tumbler in each hand he tossed the contents from one to the other. Never conveying it awry, nor spilling the least drop, he compelled the frothy liquor, as it seemed to me, to spout forth from one glass and descend into the other, in a great parabolic curve, as well-defined and calculable as a planet's orbit.

The use of tumblers rather than a shaker was standard mixing practice: the silver cocktail shaker, now inseparable from the idea of the cocktail, did not come along until 1877.

The *Police Gazette* showcased the middling sort of mixologist who flourished around the turn of the century. The weekly paper, devoted to lurid crimes, boxing, and the female form, regularly featured, along with "tonsorial experts," local bartenders from around the country, along with drink recipes sent in by mail, as many as a dozen per issue. A few paragraphs of praise for the bartender's skill would lead up to the ultimate character reference: "he is a good fellow."

The modern bartender is regarded as a kind of valet. A century ago, he was a man of substance. "In Nevada, for a time, the lawyer, the editor, the banker, the chief desperado, the chief gambler, and the saloon-keeper occupied the same level in society, and it was the highest," Mark Twain wrote in *Roughing It* (1872).

> The cheapest and easiest way to become an influential man and be looked up to by the community at large, was to stand behind a bar, wear a cluster diamond pin, and sell whiskey. I am not sure but the saloon-keeper held a shade higher rank than any other member of society. His opinion had weight. It was his privilege to say how the elections should go. No great movement could succeed without the countenance and direction of the saloon-keeper. It was a high favor when the chief saloon-keeper consented to serve in the legislature or the board of aldermen.

Some bartenders achieved celebrity status. The most famous of them all was Jerry Thomas, whose career sheds light on the profession at its higher reaches. Born in 1830 in Watertown, New York, Thomas went to sea as a young man and washed ashore in San Francisco in 1849, where he became first assistant to the principal bartender at the El Dorado. After panning for gold, he opened up a mining-town saloon and, by his own account, presented the first minstrel show in California. Returning East with his bankroll of sixteen thousand dollars, he opened up a bar under P. T. Barnum's museum in New York. Apparently, Thomas was a restless hombre. In 1853, he headed to Charleston, where he tended bar at the Mills House; then he moved west to Chicago and Saint Louis, where he served as head bartender at the Planters Hotel. Tiring of Saint Louis, Thomas headed south to New Orleans and opened a saloon, but he soon left for New York, where he became principal bartender at the Metropolitan Hotel—and patented his own brand of bitters. The best bartenders, like top chefs today, called their own tune and moved from bar to bar, from city to city, at will. So great was Thomas's renown that in 1859 he toured Europe with a four-thousand-dollar set of custom-made silver bar implements and demonstrated the American art of the cocktail to curious Londoners and Parisians.

In 1882, the *New York Sun* caught up with Thomas, by then owner of his own bar, not far from the Hoffman House. The bartender, now fifty-two, cut a curious figure, talking with the reporter as "two white rats pretty enough to be guinea pigs cut capers upon his shoulders, caressed him at the corners of his mustache, and mounted occasionally to the top of his derby hat." Nearby was the centerpiece of his art collection, a painting titled *Jerry Thomas's Dream*, showing the celebrated barman in an armchair, surrounded by famous Americans, arranged in three tiers in a kind of team picture.

Who's to say whether Thomas didn't deserve his seat among the great? To be recognized as America's greatest bartender counted for something. Standards of the profession were high. At the finer saloons, where an apprenticeship of two years was not uncommon, bartenders spent many an hour refining the visual presentation of the bar, ensuring a pleasing spectacle of sparkling glassware, attractive fruit, and clean, starched linen (a cocktail often came with a starched linen napkin for dabbing at one's mustache). Like the cocktail shaker, the cash register was a rarity until the 1880s, which perhaps accounts for the allure of the bartending profession, since the honor system allowed for robust self-tipping.

The old-time bartender probably deserved the spare change. He had to know his drinks, in an age when taste inclined toward the baroque. Consider the Gladstone cocktail, from an 1892 bar book, which called for two dashes of gum, a dash of maraschino, two dashes of bitters, one dash of absinthe, and equal parts of whiskey, Jamaica rum, and Russian kümmel. There were many others of that ilk. According to Albert Stevens Crockett, in his history of the old Waldorf bar, "certain of those bartenders knew how to make, and did make, 271 different kinds of cocktails. They knew how to compose, and did compose, 491 different kinds of mixed drinks."

The mixing of a cocktail was a matter for professionals. A man would no sooner shake one up himself than cut his own hair. Jack London had cocktails mixed up by an Oakland bartender and shipped to him in bulk. Fear of mixing created a business opportunity that the Heublein Company of Hartford seized upon with great success. In 1892, it began marketing Club Cocktails, a line of seven premixed bottled drinks (the York, Manhattan, martini, whiskey, Holland gin, Old-Tom gin, and vermouth cocktails), "scientifically blended from choicest liquors, aged and mellowed to delicious flavor and aroma." It's a dubious proposition that aging a martini improves its flavor or aroma, but perhaps scientific blending was the main selling point. The York cocktail, now forgotten, was three parts French vermouth to one part maraschino, with four dashes of orange bitters.

The original, 1862, edition of Thomas's bar book listed but ten drinks: the bottle, brandy, fancy brandy, whiskey, champagne, gin, fancy gin, Japanese, soda, and Jersey cocktails. A Japanese cocktail was brandy with orgeat (an almond syrup), bitters, and a twist of lemon; a Jersey was cider, bitters, sugar, and a twist of lemon. By the last edition, in 1887, the roster had grown to well over a hundred mixed drinks, exclusive of punches, neguses, smashes, and mulls.

The lexicographers reflect this creative explosion. Bartlett's *Dictionary of Americanisms* limits itself to a definition of the word "cocktail" in its 1859 edition. The 1877 edition lists Thomas's ten cocktails and ups the ante with another one hundred thirty drinks, among them the Ching Ching, the Deadbeat, the Deacon, the Fiscal Agent, the Moral Suasion, the Ropee, the Shambro, the Split Ticket, and the Vox Populi. And a rival lexicographer declared Bartlett's list ridiculously incomplete just twelve years later.

In his introduction to the cocktail section of his book, Thomas stated that "the cocktail is a modern invention, and is generally used on fishing and other sporting parties," which suggests that just after midcentury, the individually prepared drink served across the bar was by no means universal. And indeed, Thomas offers an entire chapter on cocktails to be bottled and taken along on outings. An ingenious product for the outdoor drinker was made by the Vinous Rubber Grape Co. of Philadelphia, which in 1885 patented rubber capsules filled with spirits or wine. The buyer popped one in his mouth, bit down for a quick, stimulating shot, and then ejected the used grape.

It is impossible to know how representative Thomas's collection of recipes is. It includes, in recognizable form, a few classics, such as the Manhattan and the Tom Collins. But they are the exceptions. Most of the drinks reflect a national sweet tooth in the gum syrup (sugar and water boiled together) added to most cocktails. When gin is called for, it is usually Old Tom gin, the sweet predecessor of the dry, London style that is universal today. Those that are not too sweet are too complicated, often calling for such obscure ingredients as arrack, orgeat, snakeroot, or tansy.

Thomas's most famous contribution to the cocktail repertoire was the Blue Blazer: equal parts Scotch and boiling water set alight and poured back and forth from one mug to another in a continuous stream of fire. The trick can be done with practice. Although the diluted whiskey barely catches fire, the reciprocal pouring acts as a kind of bellows, and the result is a roaring fire. A nineteenth-century engraving shows Thomas, arms outstretched, generating a fiery cataract some five feet in length, as three swells look on admiringly.

Dazzling but impractical, the two-tumbler method became outmoded with the invention of the cocktail shaker. The earliest patent on record was filed in 1877 by a Chicago man, who proposed a model that looks precisely like the shaker of today: a large metal cup with a screw cap and strainer.

The pyrotechnics of the American bartender and his bizarre concoctions seem to have passed unnoticed on native soil. Abroad, Uncle Sam's mixmasters created a sensation, setting up shop and stunning the Europeans with drinks like the Connecticut Eye-Opener, the Alabama Fog-Cutter, and the Lightning Smash. The names suggest that the Americans were determined to give Europe its money's worth, to assure it that the United States indeed was a wonderland of vulgar surprises.

All sorts of strange cocktails made the rounds, and most of them were on display at the Paris Exposition of 1867, where the U.S. exhibition included a genuine American bar dispensing New World concoctions, with and without alcohol. George Augustus Sala, a well-known British journalist, reported on the exposition's more memorable sights. The American bar definitely qualified.

> At the bar, and from siphon tubes decorated with silvery figures of the American eagle, were dispensed the delicious "cream soda" so highly recommended by the faculty. "Cobblers," "noggs," "smashes," "cocktails," "eye openers," "moustache twisters," and "corpse revivers" were also on hand; and I dare say you might have obtained the mystic "tip and tic," the exhilarating "morning glory," the mild but health-giving sarsaparilla punch, to say nothing of "one of them things," which is a recondite and almost inscrutable drink.

The Tip and Tic has disappeared without a trace. But the Morning Glory appears in Jerry Thomas's book, where the recipe calls for three dashes of gum syrup, two dashes of curaçao, two dashes of bitters, one dash of absinthe, one pony each of brandy and whiskey, a twist of lemon, and ice. After being stirred, strained, and topped up with soda, the mixture is stirred with a teaspoon that has a little sugar in it.

Sala may have been amused, but his countrymen took a dim view of America's contributions in the drink line. In *Cups and Their Customs*, two English writers, Henry Porter and George Roberts, deplored the "sensation drinks which have lately travelled across the Atlantic. . . . We will pass the American Bar, with its bad brandies and fiery wine, and express our gratification at the slight success which 'Pick-me-up,' 'Corpse-reviver,' 'Chain-lightning,' and the like, have had in this country."

Improbably, the Corpse Reviver did exist. It was equal parts noyau (a sweet almond liqueur), maraschino, and yellow Chartreuse, poured carefully to form three distinct bands. The drink evidently made its way across the Channel to Paris, for some thirty years later, a Cincinnatian reported strolling along the rue Auger and coming across the American Bar. Sure enough, the long list of American cocktails—among them the Bosom Caresser, Flip Flap, Heap of Comfort, and Flash of Lightning—included the well-traveled Corpse Reviver.

When the office clock is showing
That the time is half past four,
I feel I must be going
Where I've often gone before,
For I need no rough awakening,
And I want no whistle's hoot,
To say my thirst needs slaking
On the Cocktail Route.

**—From Roland Whittle, "The Cocktail Route," San
Francisco News Letter, *December 12, 1904***

The rococo cocktails that inspired English sneers did not really represent American taste. They were showpieces, for the most part, intended to astound and entertain, like the passing fads of the present-day bar—what bartenders today refer to dismissively as "umbrella drinks." The staple of most bars at the time was bourbon or rye. New York's Continental Hotel was renowned for its whiskey sours. At the Hoffman House, according to William Mulhall, the cocktails most in demand in the 1880s were the old-fashioned, the absinthe cocktail, martinis both dry and sweet, the vermouth cocktail, the Bronx, and the Turf Club (two dashes each orange bitters, maraschino, and absinthe in a glass containing equal parts French vermouth and Plymouth gin). Rum, by this time, was out of bounds, a low-rent option for the down-and-out. The pride of colonial America had become a prohibitionist expletive, and turn-of-the-century Republicans could think of no better way to promote their presidential candidate than to chant: "McKinley drinks soda water, Bryan drinks rum; McKinley is a gentleman, Bryan is a bum."

The old-time bartender nevertheless worked with a more extensive battery of flavorings and extracts than his modern-day counterpart. He had at his disposal perhaps a dozen different kinds of bitters, and the older bar books are sprinkled with such exotica as calisaya, crème de violette, and groseille syrup.

Absinthe, according to Mulhall, did not become popular until the late 1890s, but when it caught on, it created a stir. Now but a dim, lurid memory, the light-green absinthe was made by distilling an infusion of alcohol and the leaves, root, or bark of wormwood (*Artemisia absinthium*), hyssop, and mint, with angelica root, sweet flag, dittany leaves, star-anise fruit, and fennel. The result was a potent, 140-to-160-proof drink resembling Pernod. The problem was with the thujone, a fragrant ketone present in wormwood oil, which acted as a kind of hallucinogen.

The usual method of preparation was to pour a small amount of absinthe in a wineglass, then place a silver filter containing a lump of sugar over the glass. Water poured on the sugar would then drip sweetly into the bitter absinthe. The effects of frequent use can be seen in any number of Impressionist paintings. "People were afraid of it," noted Mulhall, "and many fearful stories were told of its effects on French drinkers. But it was too seductive to be barred." He served it in a dozen different cocktails, the most popular being Absinthe Frappé, Absinthe Panache, Absinthe California, and Absinthe Drip.

Mulhall claimed that the celebrated Manhattan cocktail, long a rival to the martini, was invented by a man named Black, who kept a saloon ten doors below Houston Street on Broadway. This runs counter to the more popular theory that the drink was created at the Manhattan Club in 1874, at a banquet to celebrate Governor William J. Tilden's electoral victory. The club's official history simply asserts that the cocktail was invented on its premises, providing no date, and then provides the recipe: equal parts whiskey and vermouth, plus orange bitters, which has evolved over time to the modern formulation of two parts whiskey to one part vermouth, with Angostura bitters. (The disappearance of orange bitters is a sad footnote in the history of American drink.)

If the club is sketchy on the Manhattan, it does build up a certain credibility by citing a slew of other cocktails first created at the club's bar: the Sam Ward (yellow Chartreuse with a twist of lemon); the Frappé New Orleans à la Graham (whiskey, mint, and sugar); the Royal Cup (a pint of champagne, a quart of Bordeaux, soda, one pony each of brandy and maraschino, lemon juice, sugar, mint, fruits in season, and a cucumber); the Manhattan cocktail à la Gilbert (whiskey, French vermouth, and Amer Picon bitters); the Manhattan Cooler à la McGregor (Scotch, soda, lemon juice, and sugar); the Columbus (whiskey, calisaya, orange bitters, acid phosphate, and a dash of curaçao); the Brut (vermouth, orange bitters, acid phosphate, and maraschino); the Riding Club (calisaya, lemon juice, and Angostura bitters); the Racquet (gin, vermouth, orange bitters, and crème de cacao); the Star (applejack, vermouth, yellow Chartreuse, and cherry bounce); the Queen Anne (brandy, vermouth, orange bitters, and maraschino); the Plimpton (Jamaica rum, vermouth, and Angostura bitters); and the Smithtown (whiskey, vermouth, lemon juice, and orange bitters). "Indeed, the Club has drinks for every day in the year, Sundays included; for all seasons, and national, State, and city festivals."

Whatever its origin, the Manhattan seems to have reigned supreme at the Hoffman House. It came in an infinite number of varieties, and bartenders had to keep track of special formulas required by regular customers. It was the drink of the substantial man. Downtown at the Waldorf, J. Pierpont Morgan ordered one every day after the stock market closed.

Most of the classic cocktails, including the martini, the Manhattan, the old-fashioned, and the Bronx, were born in this high-living, fecund era. The Bronx cocktail, if Albert Stevens Crockett, in his *Old Waldorf Bar Days*, is to be believed, was invented by Johnny Solon at the Waldorf Hotel, which opened in 1897. Solon recalled that he was making up a Duplex—equal parts French and Italian vermouth, shaken up with squeezed orange peel and two dashes of orange bitters—when a customer challenged him to make a new cocktail. Solon mixed one part orange juice to three parts gin and, inspired by the Duplex, threw in a dash each of French and Italian vermouth. Solon said he named the drink the Bronx because he had recently visited the Bronx zoo.

Whoever invented it, the drink took off. "The Bronx was fashionable," Bernard DeVoto later wrote in *The Hour.*

> The gay dogs of the Murray Hill Age drank it, the boulevardiers who wore boaters with a string to the left lapel and winked at Gibson Girls as far up Fifth Avenue as 59th Street. It had the same cachet that Maxim's had, or Delmonico's, or say the splendid Richard Harding Davis at the more splendid Knickerbocker bar, or O. Henry in his cellar restaurant, or the bearded (or Van Dyke-ed) critics of Park Row.

DeVoto did not like the Bronx. It was the first cocktail to use fruit juice, and fruit juice, he believed, was a bad influence on drink. In his view, the only thing to be said in favor of the Bronx was that it was not as bad as the Orange Blossom, also known as the Algonquin (equal parts orange juice and gin). G. Selmer Fougner, in his "Along the Wine Trail" column for the *New York Sun*, theorized that Prohibition killed the Bronx through overuse. Everyone had gin, everyone had orange juice, and by the 1930s everyone was sick of the combination.

Most cocktails of the period have not survived. Their very names, in many cases, suggest a limited shelf life. The cocktail instantly registered events of the moment, celebrities, hit shows, racehorses, and the passing enthusiasms of the average man. When Peary reached the South Pole, his exploit inspired the Arctic cocktail. Broadway plays and musicals like *The Merry Widow, The Chocolate Soldier, Trilby*, and *Zaza* demanded their own drinks. The Metropole and the Normandie, New York hotels, had drinks named after them, as did the Bijou, a Broadway theater. The Rob Roy began with the play of the same name, while the Free Silver Fizz recalls William Jennings Bryan's political platform favoring a silver-backed currency. The Dorlando commemorated an American marathon runner in the 1908 Olympic Games.

Yale, Harvard, Princeton, and Cornell had their own cocktails, now forgotten. The Clover Club, a survivor, was the property of a club of the same name, which met at the Bellevue Hotel in Philadelphia. The Ward 8 sounds sinister but commemorates the festivities when members of Boston's Hedricks Club, a political operation ruled by Martin "The Mahatma" Lomasney, gathered at the Locke-Ober Café in 1898 to celebrate their man's certain election to the state legislature from the eighth ward the following day.

Sometimes the inspiration for a cocktail was pure silliness. A shortlived fad drink of the 1880s, the White Plush, came into being, according to the *New York Herald*, when a dry-goods buyer from New England went out for a night on the town in New York with two suppliers. Wary of being plied with drink, he insisted on ordering milk and seltzer, to which the bartender, tipped off by a wink from his companions, added a dash of whiskey. As the evening wore on, the milks kept coming, with the whiskey assuming a larger proportion and the seltzer left out entirely. At one point, the buyer tipped over his glass, watched the white liquid spread over the table, and murmured reflectively, "Gosh, it looks like white plush, don't it?" Or so the story goes. Students of barroom etymology, beware.

New York supplied a disproportionate number of new cocktails—or at least its bartenders bragged louder and more journalists were around to record their claims. But New Orleans, with a mere fraction of New York's population, contributed mightily to the development of the cocktail. Antoine Peychaud, mixing up bitters in his apothecary shop—in a building still standing, at 437 Royal Street—may or may not have been the father of the cocktail. Indisputably, New Orleans gave birth to the Sazerac and the Ramos Gin Fizz. Both drinks are solid classics, full equals of the old-fashioned and the mint julep, yet they await rediscovery. The third drink associated with the city, the Dripped Absinthe Frappé, served at the Old Absinthe House, is now but a folk memory.

The Sazerac was created at 13 Exchange Alley, in a bar owned by John B. Schiller, the local agent for the brandies of Sazerac-de-Forge et Fils in Angoulême, France. In 1859, Schiller opened his bar, naming it the Sazerac Coffee House. The brandy cocktails he served apparently caught on, but they underwent changes over the years. Rye replaced the cognac, and a dash of absinthe was added for interest. When the law decided that absinthe was a little too interesting, a local substitute was developed: herbsaint.

The Ramos Gin Fizz was born when Henry C. Ramos arrived in New Orleans in 1888 and bought the Imperial Cabinet Saloon (he later moved to the Stag Saloon, opposite the St. Charles Hotel). The drink, which calls for powdered sugar, a few drops of orange-flower water, lemon and lime juice, gin, egg white, cream, and seltzer, depends on vigorous shaking for several minutes to achieve the proper ethereal lightness. It is said that during Mardi Gras as many as thirty-five boys could be seen shaking up fizzes at Ramos's establishment.

Lafcadio Hearn, the idiosyncratic New Orleans literary critic, took a special interest in the food and drink of his native city, going so far as to open his own restaurant, with all items on the menu priced at a nickel. The venture failed when his partner absconded with the cash. But in 1885, Hearn turned his culinary knowledge to account in *La Cuisine Créole*, which contains recipes and observations on the New Orleans way of drink. Although Hearn lists gin fizzes, absinthe drinks galore, and assorted juleps, punches, and pousse-cafés, his heart belongs to the brûlé, a flaming punch served after dinner. Hearn, whose imagination ran naturally to chiaroscuro, loved the ritual of the brûlé: The lights would be lowered, and a silver bowl would make its way to the center of the table, casting ghoulish light on the faces of the diners. In the bowl was a punch of French brandy, kirsch, maraschino, cinnamon, and allspice, to be transferred to glasses in a ladle filled with brandy-soaked sugar cubes. A petit brûlé, for one person, was concocted in the hollowed-out half of an orange, whose seared skin added piquancy to the brew.

The only city to rival New Orleans was San Francisco, whose grand hotels of the gaslight era could rival the best New York had to offer. The city's better bars formed a seductive chain known as the Cocktail Route, which began at the Reception Saloon on Sutter Street and wound its way to upper Market Street. San Francisco's principal contribution to the mixed drink was Pisco Punch, invented at the Bank Exchange in the 1870s. Pisco brandy is distilled from the sweet muscat grape in South America. The best examples came from near the port of Pisco in Peru. Thomas W. Knox wrote: "It is perfectly colorless, quite fragrant, very seductive, terribly strong, and has a flavor somewhat resembling Scotch whisky, but much more delicate with a marked fruity taste." Knox describes drinking it hot, with lemon and nutmeg. Another drink associated with the Bank Exchange was Button Punch, which used Pisco brandy too. The drink has long been forgotten, but Rudyard Kipling was treated to a sample—perhaps several samples—in 1899. The punch made an impression. "It is the highest and noblest product of the age," Kipling wrote. "I have a theory it is compounded of cherub's wings, the glory of a tropical dawn, the red clouds of sunset, and the fragments of lost epics by dead masters." That is to say, it went down easy.

With Prohibition, the golden age of the cocktail came to a crashing halt. It was too good to last, and Americans seemed to recognize the fact. The saloon went out with a whimper, and the night of January 16, 1920, saw a resigned, peaceful America segue into Prohibition. Wakes were held in cities throughout the land, and some bars gave out miniature coffins as souvenirs. At the Park Avenue Hotel in New York, a casket was filled with black bottles. But the riotous send-off the police were expecting never materialized.

The mood was one of regret and resignation. The great bars, the grand hotels, the splendid cocktails—all of them vanished overnight, as though whisked away by an incantation. "The Bamboo Cocktails at the Holland House," lamented one writer, so forlorn that he could only list his losses, "the Jack Roses at Eberlin's, the two for a quarter Manhattans at the Knickerbocker bar, the Thomas Flyers at Sherry's, the Infuriators at the Beaux Arts, the Orange Blossoms at the Manhattan, the Central Park Souths at the Plaza, the Absinthe Drips at Murray's, the Silver Fizzes at the Waldorf, the Perfect Cocktails at Delmonico's, the Old Fashioneds at the Imperial, the Mint Juleps at the Astor, the Diamond Fizzes at the Belmont, the Rickeys at Captain Church's, the Clover Clubs at the Buckingham, the Bronxes at the Holland House, the mint drinks at the Green Turtle, the Gin Daisies at Rector's, the Whiskey Sours at Burns's"—it was over, forever.

THE JAZZ AGE

7

Turkey Cocktail:
To one large turkey add one gallon
of vermouth and a demijohn
of Angostura bitters. Shake.

—The Notebooks of F. Scott Fitzgerald

When William Powell makes his debut as Nick Charles in *The Thin Man,* he's first seen as an anonymous figure off to the right of the screen, vigorously working a silver cocktail shaker near the bar of the Normandie Hotel. Gradually, the moving camera threads its way through the crowd toward the bar, and Charles comes into full view. It turns out that while shaking, he is propounding his theory on the right way to mix a martini. "The important thing is the rhythm," he says, slurring his words. "A Manhattan should be shaken to a fox trot, the Bronx to a two-step, but a dry martini must always be shaken to a waltz. Mind you, there's a still more modern trend—" But the new trend remains a mystery. Enter Nora Charles, fresh from Christmas shopping, pulled by Asta on a leash and peeved at missing out on the drinks. She immediately orders five martinis. Cut to the Charles bedroom next morning: Nora recumbent with an ice bag on her head, as her husband and her dog look on solicitously.

The Thin Man appeared in 1934, the year that it became legal for Americans to drink again. But its ethos is soaked, so to speak, in the cocktail atmosphere of Prohibition, a pointless fourteen-year exercise that proved, at great expense to the taxpayer, the rather obvious truth that if citizens are deprived of legal liquor, they will seek out illegal liquor. Once Congress had passed the Eighteenth Amendment and the Volstead Act, which put it into effect, the saloon gave way, immediately, to the speakeasy, sparking a revolution in taste and manners. To the sound of a thousand chattering cocktail shakers, women stepped right up to the brass rail and drank with the men. Gin was king, and the fun began.

The 1920s shine in the popular imagination today as the cocktail years, given double luster by the sleek, glossy surface of American culture. With Europe devastated and profoundly demoralized by war, America, rich and confident, stepped into the center of history's spotlight, impossibly glamorous, stylish, and, above all, modern. As the stock market soared, America rushed full tilt into the age of the automobile and the skyscraper, while the great democratic cultural forms—the movie, the animated cartoon, the comic strip, and jazz— achieved a state of perfection virtually overnight. In industry and the arts, America radiated confidence and energy. The nation was in a festive mood.

The 1920s now seem as much a tempo as anything else. The cocktail shaker was the metronome for a decade when everything was fast. In the speeded-up world of the newsreel and the silent film, it was a natural transition from the frantic back-and-forth of a cocktail shaker to the rapid steps of the Charleston and the double-time milling and frantic arm-waving on the floor of the stock exchange.

Conventional wisdom has it that Prohibition did not work, that Americans drank more during the Jazz Age than ever before. This is not quite true. Overall, the country was drinking a little less by the time Prohibition limped toward the finish line, but the national trend had been downward anyway. Those who *did* drink, however, drank more, and they gravitated toward hard liquor, the bootlegger's choice: it was easier to make, more compact, and less detectable than beer or wine. Prohibition, in other words, turned a lot of beer and wine drinkers into whiskey drinkers.

Prohibition not only changed what Americans drank; it also changed the way they drank. It put a nudge and a wink into the experience. It encouraged the massive binge, the hangover worn as a badge of honor, the hip flask displayed as a naughty signal that the bearer belonged to a rather daring fraternity. Because a drink was denied by law, those who did drink were determined to do it up right when the opportunity arose. After penetrating the inner sanctum of a speakeasy, what was the point of sipping tentatively? Especially if you were in town for only a few days. This was the era that coined the phrase "to make whoopee." And whoopee required effort—it didn't make itself. Americans put a lot of work into their fun. Moreover, something in the air—the same mysterious ingredient that inspired flagpole sitting and goldfish swallowing—encouraged recklessness. "Take three chorus girls and three men," ran one facetious recipe from the 1920s, "soak in champagne till midnight, squeeze into an automobile. Add a dash of joy, and a drunken chauffeur. Shake well. Serve at 70 miles an hour. Chaser: a coroner's inquest."

Much of the heat in the battle between wets and dries was generated by moral friction between the city and the country. From the vantage point of a Kansas farm, places like Chicago and Saint Louis looked like stewpots of licentiousness. The Eighteenth Amendment helped turn myth into reality. In New York especially, Prohibition did not prohibit. "Back in 1920," F. Scott Fitzgerald wrote, "I shocked a rising young businessman by suggesting a cocktail before lunch. In 1929 there was liquor in half the downtown offices, and liquor in half the large buildings." The transformation got under way literally overnight. In accordance with the Volstead Act, passed the previous year, prohibition commenced at 12:01 A.M. on January 17, 1920. The next day, the 50-50 Club opened over a garage at 129 West 50th Street in New York city, launched by fifty members who paid one hundred dollars each for the privilege of keeping whiskey in lockers. There was no bar. The practice spread quickly, as concerned citizens took action with a sense of purpose not seen since the colonists organized resistance to the laws of England.

For most Americans, it was a quiet, sneaking sort of revolt. More than ever, a man's home was his castle, a fortress to keep the influence of Prohibition at bay. In olden days, liquor stayed in the local saloon, far from the eyes of wife and children. If pressed, Dad did his drinking on the sly, stealing a nip from a pint bottle under the stairs. Now, as a practical matter, most drinking, and a fair amount of distilling, was done at home. Suddenly, mixing a mean cocktail became one of the manly arts, like carving the holiday turkey. This new development set off a boom in the bar-accoutrement industry. One magazine writer, strolling through a department store, noted that it sold twelve styles of silver cocktail glasses, twenty-three of glass, fourteen models of cocktail shakers, and eighteen kinds of hip flask; "there were innumerable different kinds of wine glasses, champagne glasses, and so many kinds of whiskey glasses I lost count." Some companies produced nonalcoholic Bronx, martini, and Manhattan cocktails, to which alcohol could be added.

Hundreds of legitimate restaurants and night spots folded almost immediately, deprived of their biggest source of income. New York's most celebrated street instantly lost its sparkle as, one by one, the grand hotels, the legendary bars, the splendid restaurants, shut their doors. "Broadway faded into a street of cafeterias, electric shoe-shining stands, nut shoppes, physical-culture demonstrators and five-cent dance halls," wrote the Broadway columnist Joseph Sobol, "as the gates to an invisible paradise in the Fifties along Fifth and Park avenues sucked away the silk-hat and ermine crowd."

A few speakeasies really did live up to the romantic notion of whispered passwords, secret hutches and trapdoors, false entrances, and unimaginable splendor within. "Some speakeasies are disguised behind florists' shops, or behind undertakers' coffins," noted a French visitor to New York. "I know one, right in Broadway, which is entered through an imitation telephone box." Membership cards were more common than passwords, which tended to be of the "Joe sent me" variety. But peepholes really did exist. "Key clubs" issued regular patrons with their own keys. Jack and Charlie's, which later evolved into the "21" Club, introduced a shrewd bit of evasive technology: its bar was outfitted with an emergency button that caused the liquor shelves to flip their bottles down a shaft to the basement, leaving nothing but broken glass and a suspicious aroma.

The better nightclubs and speakeasies cast a kind of spell in the 1920s. They became inseparable from the overall atmosphere of fun, what Fitzgerald called the "general decision to be amused," and decades later, old speakeasy hands would intone the honor roll of bygone Manhattan night spots, beginning with Texas Guinan's and the Kit-Kat and winding up with the Marlborough House, the

Hi Hat, the Ha-Ha Club, the Stork Club, and 21 West 52nd—now the "21" Club.

The glorious profession of the bartender suffered a fatal blow, however. Prohibition sent dozens of mixologists across the ocean to ply their trade at "American bars" all over Europe.

Back home, the more daring bartenders continued to ply their trade illegally; the rest found new lines of work or, perhaps even more depressingly, stepped sideways into legitimate work at hotels and restaurants, like the spectral bartender in Fitzgerald's "The Rich Boy," who wound up chilling nonalcoholic champagne at the Plaza Hotel.

For anyone who could compound a drink, there was no trouble finding a job. The first New York bar serving mixed drinks, as opposed to pouring straight from the bottle, opened in 1922 in a brownstone on Fortieth Street east of Fifth Avenue. Before, nervous speakeasy owners wanted the option, in case of a raid, of putting the bottles in the overcoat pockets of their customers. Then they could claim they were only serving "setups"—glasses, ice, and club soda or ginger ale.

The setup quickly became an institution. At many restaurants and clubs, the waiter would bring over a tray with ice, glasses, and bottles of White Rock soda and then turn away discreetly as customers reached for their flasks and poured. (It was considered bad form to leave a flask in plain sight on the table.) The soft-drink companies made no effort whatever to disguise the new market their product had found: suddenly, print advertisements showed tuxedoed young blades in nightclubs eyeing, with suspicious enthusiasm, the little bottles of ginger ale offered by a waiter in black tie.

The Eighteenth Amendment made for some interesting legal arguments. Early on, a hapless bank president in Chicago found himself the subject of a precedent-setting case in the early days of Prohibition, when he was arrested for possession of a hip flask. A U.S. District Court was asked to decide whether his trousers were legally a vehicle and should be confiscated and sold at auction like an automobile.

Prices rose. The standard had been two for a quarter; good whiskey ran ten to fifteen cents a shot. At the swank Waldorf bar, a cocktail cost twenty cents. With Prohibition, the base price in speakeasies became forty to eighty cents and rose from there to three dollars in the more luxurious spots.

New York City seemed to have a monopoly on the swanky joints. Before Prohibition, the city was already firmly established as the national capital of entertainment, fine dining, and sophisticated fun. Against the odds, the nightlife tradition lived on. While other towns made do with thrown-together speakeasies, or "blind pigs," Gotham offered (along with plenty of clip joints and dumps) palaces of food, music, and illicit drink.

The top speakeasies, located in posh mansions, served food prepared by a chef from one of the great hotels put out of business by Prohibition. A top-of-the-line speak might boast two bars, a dance floor, Ping-Pong and backgammon rooms, lounges, an art gallery, and a band.

"Dark and guarded doors opened into a spreading world of enchantment," wrote Joseph Sobol, "a world of soft lights, seductive scents, silken music, adroit entertainment, smoke and laughter, of perfection of food and service, of wines and liquors of the first quality, all in a setting of gold and silver and brocade, velvet, iron, glass, and exotic woods."

The Park Avenue Club in New York, designed by Joseph Urban, had an octagonal bar surrounded by floor-to-ceiling mirrors. At the

Merry-Go-Round (146–148 East 56th Street), customers hopped onto plaster horses and rotated with the bar, which made a complete circuit every eleven minutes. At the Country Club on Park Avenue, patrons could play Ping-Pong and miniature golf. The Aquarium served drinks like the Goldfish cocktail: equal parts Goldwasser liqueur, gin, and French vermouth. "The kingfish is the lobster who runs up the largest check, even though he gets stewed to the gills," wrote a wisecracking journalist in *Manhattan*, a short-lived publication, whose series "Behind the Brownstone Front" profiled one "giggle-water parlor" a week.

The top speaks made it easy to run up the bill. Customers could pay a dollar for a special ten-pack of Camels, two dollars for a pitcher of water or a tiny bottle of White Rock club soda, ten dollars for a pint of whiskey, and twenty-five dollars for a bottle of champagne. The cover charge at Texas Guinan's ran twenty dollars and up.

The crème de la crème was the Marlborough House. Prospective clients were led into a sealed wood vestibule, where they pressed a pearl push button and presented their credentials. On the first floor, French wall benches in silver leather ran the length of walls that were scarlet up to the wainscoting and silver up to the ceiling. White storks with scarlet beaks were displayed on the walls. The cabaret room on the second floor was decorated in royal blue and copper, with dozens of mirrors and a ceiling of hammered brass. An orchestra provided entertainment, and patrons were entertained by torch singers and "Egyptian" magicians.

Competing for the well-heeled customer the speakeasies spent lavishly on food and entertainment. The drinks were always an uncertain affair. But the pleasurable mix of cocktails, dinner, a floor show, and dancing proved durable, and the speakeasy of the twenties, without missing a beat, became the nightclub of the thirties, forties, and fifties.

Women liked the new setup. No speakeasy could afford to segregate by gender, so for once, they got to go along. "The old days when father spent his evenings at Cassidy's bar with the rest of the boys are gone, and probably gone forever," wrote the journalist Elmer Davis. "Cassidy may still be in business at the old stand and father may still go down there of evenings, but since Prohibition, mother goes down with him." This feature of Prohibition stayed on after repeal, and it represents the one positive contribution of the Eighteenth Amendment. Women civilized the saloon, not by closing it down, but by ordering their drinks alongside the men.

Like most all-male institutions, the sawdust-strewn temple, with its spittoons and mildly prurient canvases, was an obstacle to social progress. It was, in truth, juvenile, a grown-up version of the backyard clubhouse with "No Girls Allowed" painted across the door. It reinforced a sexual apartheid that was already falling apart at the turn of the century, a victim of its own contradictions. Predictably, the men grumbled, but more perhaps out of a sense of duty than from actual conviction. Don Marquis, in *Her Foot Is on the Brass Rail*, offered a comic lament for the old barroom, but the work lacks bite: the easy social mingling of the speakeasy, and the legal cocktail lounges that it spawned, were too obviously an improvement on the old institution.

The liquor changed, and so did the drinks. America had been a whiskey-drinking nation, and throughout Prohibition it waged a doomed struggle to remain one. Canadian whiskey and Scotch made their way into the country by a thousand illegal channels, and the substantial reservoir of legal whiskey relabeled "For Medicinal Purposes Only" somehow migrated from doctors' offices to the open market. None of it remained intact. One bottle of good whiskey would be stretched with homemade hooch to make four or five bottles. The days of drinking straight whiskey were over. Rye whiskey and ginger ale became a staple of the twenties and thirties, causing sales of the soft drink to nearly double between 1920 and 1928. When Garbo first spoke on the screen, in *Anna Christie*, the earth moved. The lines were: "Gimme a viskey, ginger ale on the side, and don't be stingy, baby."

"Everyone was drinking, or had just finished a drink, or was just about to take one," O'Hara wrote of a country club party in *Appointment in Samarra*.

> The drinks were rye and ginger ale, practically unanimously, except for a few highballs of applejack and White Rock or apple and ginger ale, or gin and ginger ale. Only a few of the inner sanctum members were drinking Scotch. The liquor, that is, the rye, was all about the same: most people bought drug store rye on prescriptions (the physicians who were club members saved "scrips" for their patients), and cut it with alcohol and colored water. It was not poisonous, and it got you tight, which was all that was required of it and all that could be said for it.

But whiskey is a difficult flavor to counterfeit. The quickest and easiest spirit to produce was gin—a despised, low-rent spirit ever since the days of Hogarth—and thousands of Americans learned how. The standard method was to add oil of juniper to a mixture of 40 percent alcohol and 60 percent water—*et voilà!*— "The gin is aged," wrote one post-repeal bar book, "about the length of time it takes to get from the bathroom where it is made to the front porch where the cocktail party is in progress." Gin was simple, gin was quick. Once the down-and-outer's choice, it became the spirit of the age.

Drinks fell into two categories: quick-and-easy, for fast intake, and thick-and-sweet, to disguise the poor quality of the base spirit. For the less stouthearted, bad liquor demanded sweet, heavy mixers. Prohibition launched a thousand alcoholic milk shakes that can curdle the blood even at a distance of sixty years. The most famous was the Alexander, a noisome mixture of gin, crème de cacao, and cream. Nearly as bad was the Cowboy: Scotch and cream over ice.

Johnny Brooks, in *My 35 Years Behind Bars,* gave a fair idea of how the typical Prohibition bartender plied his trade. To his credit, Brooks was humble even in his boasting. "I've invented a lot of mixed drinks in my time," he said. "Some of them are known all over the country now and have become standard drinks. And some of them are not so well known, probably because they're not such good drinks." Brooks turned vague when it came to those drinks "known all over the country," halfheartedly taking credit only for the Between the Sheets (equal parts brandy, Bacardi, Cointreau, and lemon juice) but expressing a willingness to back off if challenged. He staked his claim to history on something called the Cubanola, which he shook up for the first time in 1925 while tending bar in Westchester County, New York. "Someone came in," he wrote, "and ordered a Bacardi cocktail. The bootleg Bacardi we had wasn't the real stuff, and it was raw. I decided to doctor it up a bit." Desperately trying to cover up the rum, Brooks moved back and forth between sweet and sour ingredients, adding grenadine, orange juice, pineapple juice, lemon juice, and, finally, egg white for eye appeal. There it was—the Cubanola, which no one has ordered or heard of since. And so it was with a thousand creations of the so-called cocktail age, a designation that makes sense only if quantity is the criterion.

For Americans who broke under the strain, there was always Havana. No sooner had Prohibition become a dead certainty than steamship companies began outfitting vessels for an overnight Florida-to-

Cuba service. One Newark bartender moved his entire establishment, right down to the barstools. Americans who made the trip discovered rum again, most of them at the Florida bar on Montserrat Street, where the legendary Constantino poured the daiquiris that Hemingway made famous.

The daiquiri was not a new drink. It had been created in the late nineteenth century and named for the village of the same name, located near Santiago—and, it so happens, the Bacardi distillery. The inventor appears to have been an American engineer named Jennings Cox, who managed the properties of the Spanish-American Iron Co. and the Pennsylvania Steel Co. in Cuba. According to Linda Wolfe, who tracked down Cox's granddaughter for her *Cooking of the Caribbean Islands,* Cox received some important American guests in the summer of 1896 but found that he had run out of gin. Wary of serving straight rum, he added lime juice and sugar. This was the cocktail equivalent of "Watson, I hear you"—a stunning breakthrough, all the more wondrous for its simplicity.

Among the clippings that Cox's granddaughter saved is the testimonial of Admiral Lucius Johnson, who served in the Spanish-American War and had the good fortune to run into Cox and his daiquiris. Johnson and his men took plenty of rum, and the daiquiri recipe, back with them to the United States and introduced the cocktail to the Army and Navy Club in Washington, D.C., an event commemorated by a brass plaque in the club's Daiquiri Lounge. With this foothold on the mainland, the daiquiri found its way into bars across the United States.

Havana had more than the daiquiri to offer. Tourists were also ordering Presidentes (equal parts Bacardi rum and French vermouth, with a dash of curaçao or grenadine) and Mary Pickfords (fresh pineapple juice and Bacardi rum, with a dash of grenadine). But it was the daiquiri that ruled, and over the decades made El Floridita a close contender with Harry's New York Bar in Paris for the title of the most famous bar in the world.

Hemingway, of course, had a lot to do with putting the Floridita on the map. The bar had existed in one form or another since 1820, when it was called La Piña de Plata—The Silver Pineapple. With a nod to the new political reality, it became El Florida after the Spanish-American War, or, affectionately, El Floridita. But it was just another bar until Hemingway walked in and wrapped a large paw around a sugarless frozen daiquiri, the creation of Constantino Ribailagua, a Catalonian who had begun working there in 1914. In the 1930s and 1940s, Hemingway and the "Wild Daiquiri" achieved a seamless unity. He commonly worked his way through about a dozen of these lime slurpees, often ordering doubles, which became known as Papa Dobles. A. E. Hotchner's biography of Hemingway gives the recipe as two and a half jiggers Bacardi White Label, the juice of two limes and half a grapefruit, and six drops of maraschino liqueur, blended with shaved ice in a mixer and served in large goblets.

The fruit of Hemingway's barroom labors is the daiquiri's unforgettable cameo appearance in *Islands in the Stream*, the finest description of a drink in American literature. The painter Thomas Hudson, drinking one of Hemingway's patented frozen daiquiris, takes a good look in the glass "at the clear part below the frappéd top." The daiquiri "reminded him of the sea. The frappéd part of the drink was like the wake of a ship and the clear part was the way the water looked when the bow cut it when you were in shallow water over marl bottom. That was almost the exact color." Only a man who drank deeply, and thought deeply as he drank, gazing at marl bottom about five inches from the end of his nose, could have written these lines.

Hemingway's massive presence brought luster—not to mention a whopping tab—to any bar. Understandably, any number of drinking establishments claimed his patronage, just as all eighteenth-century houses between Virginia and New York suggest a connection with George Washington. La Bodeguita del Medio hung a sign at the bar purporting to be a quote from Hemingway: "My daiquiri at the Floridita. My mojito at the Bodeguita." The alleged endorsement gave undeniable cachet to the mojito, a kind of rum mint julep, but the evidence seems a little shaky that Hemingway ever set foot in the place. There is no question about the Floridita, where Hemingway's favorite barstool has been retired, like a baseball uniform.

The best of the old Prohibition bars still echo faintly with old voices, recalling those heroic days when a cocktail was an act of defiance, a blow struck for civilized values, the urban citizen's rebuff to Bible Belt tyranny. The state decreed that man would be virtuous; the rattling cocktail shakers at a hundred thousand bars said otherwise.

Not surprisingly, the Noble Experiment ended with a whimper. In the course of fourteen years, Americans had spent an estimated $36 billion on bootleg liquor, and the government had not a penny of excise-tax money to show for it. With the United States in the depths of economic depression, the jobs and revenue that a legal drink industry would generate looked doubly attractive. Enforcement of Prohibition had become a bad joke. It was time to call it a day. Beer and wine became legal as of midnight, April 7, 1933. On December 5 of the same year, the Eighteenth Amendment was repealed: the manufacture and consumption of beverage alcohol, including spirits, was again legal in the United States.

RECONSTRUCTION
8

During the era of bathtub gin and bootleg whiskey, there grew to manhood and womanhood a new generation. . . . Their idea of hospitality, in many instances, is to place a full cocktail shaker, a full bottle of rye or Scotch before their guests and let them entertain themselves.

–Julien J. Proskauer, What'll You Have? (1933)

With the legal cocktail back in business, life became simpler, and so did the drinks. "A general return to reason has done away with most of the exotic drinks," the author of *The Gun Club Drink Book* (1939) noted approvingly. He then banished virtually all of them with the dictum "A real cocktail is short and snappy."

The newly founded *Esquire*, arbiter of male taste, lost no time in proclaiming the cocktail standards for post-repeal America. It rolled out "The 10 Best Cocktails of 1934." Some were bona fide classics: the old-fashioned, the dry martini, the Ward 8, the daiquiri, the vermouth cassis, and the champagne cocktail. Others were newcomers: Planters Punch, the old-fashioned Dutch (an old-fashioned made with genever, or Dutch gin), and the Harvest Moon (two parts apple-

jack to one-half part lime juice and one-half part orgeat). The tenth
drink on the list, the vodka cocktail, resonates eerily: In 1934, virtually no one had ever heard of the spirit that today outsells all others
in the United States.

At the same time, *Esquire* waved goodbye to "the pansies"—the ten
worst cocktails of the previous decade: the Bronx, the Alexander, the
Pousse-Café, the Sweetheart, the Orange Blossom, the Pink Lady, the
Clover Club, the Fluffy Ruffles, the Pom Pom, and the Cream Fizz.
The names alone relegate most of these concoctions to cocktail hell.
But why the Bronx should have offended so many so often remains
puzzling today. Bernard DeVoto singled it out for a literary pistol-
whipping in the 1940s, and as late as the 1950s, a *Time* magazine
writer found it necessary to administer a few extra kicks to its pros-
trate form, calling it "a desecration of the martini, a cheerless drink
now well on its way to oblivion." The Bronx was the Bukharin of
cocktails, denounced with unseemly enthusiasm as the Stalinist or-
thodoxy of the martini rigidified.

With the 1930s, America settled down. The overheated inventiveness of the Jazz Age cooled, the frantic rattling of the shaker gave way
to the gentle clinking of ice cubes in a highball glass, and peace
settled over the land. After sifting through the bar book of the old
Waldorf, one writer found that only 11 of its 513 drinks had survived.
And America was not in the mood to replenish them. Mencken considered this a sign of mental health. "The same sound instinct that
prompts the more enlightened minority of mankind to come in out of
a thunderstorm," he wrote, "has also taught it to confine its day-in and
day-out boozing to about a dozen standard varieties—the martini, the
Manhattan, the daiquiri, the sidecar, the orange blossom, the Alexander, the Bronx, and a few others."

Every aspect of drinking was becoming standardized. In the years of Prohibition, America had revolutionized the techniques of advertising. Now, with lavish print campaigns, the giant distilling companies could establish national brands in a matter of months—most of them unheard of before Prohibition. Chicken Cock and Green River bourbons, Sunny Brook and Susquehanna ryes, soon disappeared, their places taken by newcomers like Seagram's Seven Crown, Crown Royal, and Four Roses. Picturesque local labels were bought up by the big companies and retired. Almost unnoticed, rye whiskey disappeared from the American scene. Once dominant in the Northeast, it became the quaint choice of a few old-timers. This was a drastic loss, since the substitution of bourbon for rye has grossly distorted the flavor of dozens of cocktails, chief among them the Manhattan.

The distilling industry underwent a drastic consolidation and was soon dominated by four giant companies. The cocktail, following suit, soon came to mean a mere handful of drinks. Most people settled for a highball (whiskey or gin on the rocks with soda), about the laziest cocktail in existence, with Scotch taking precedence over rye beginning in the mid-1930s. The slightly more adventurous collins, a highball plus lemon and sugar, gave the pink slip to all manner of fizzes, rickeys, and bucks.

Drinking became less interesting. One of the few cocktails that the decade produced was the multi-rum Zombie, a heat-seeking missile that, after achieving a brief burst of popularity, managed to linger on and find a place in the permanent repertoire. Lucius Beebe, the famous bon vivant, said he first encountered the drink at Trader Vic's restaurant in California (Trader Vic himself credited Don the Beachcomber, a Los Angeles restaurateur) but traced the drink's popularity to the 1939 New York World's Fair, where it was served at the Hurricane Bar. The distinction is a dubious one. At the opposite extreme was the splendid but not very original gin and tonic, made possible after Canada Dry developed a bottled quinine beverage.

As in the arts, the pendulum in drinking fashion swings back and forth between simplicity and refinement, classicism and romanticism. Periods of frenetic creativity, initially productive, end in excessive ornamentation and even decadence. The inevitable next step is a return to order, an insistence on classical virtues of simplicity, integrity, and restraint.

Bernard DeVoto declared that "there are only two cocktails." They are: "a slug of whiskey" poured over ice with perhaps a touch of Angostura bitters, or even a twist of orange or lemon peel; and the martini, in a ratio of 3.7 to 1, no olive. In other words, a century and a half of inspired work brought the cocktail full circle, back to the frontiersman's bittered sling, plus the martini.

But the reaction was as extreme as the excesses of the 1920s. It is possible that once Americans were given the chance to shake 'em up with decent liquor again, they simply had forgotten what the real stuff tasted like, or what a crack bartender could do with the right ingredients. The problem wasn't limited to drink. Prohibition and the Depression virtually annihilated fine dining in America. The great gastronomic temples like Delmonico's and Maxim's quickly collapsed when alcohol became illegal, and their sophistication and European flair did not return for at least half a century. The exuberance and professionalism of the grand gin palaces disappeared along with the twelve-course dinner.

A rather sad document in this regard is Patrick Gavin Duffy's *Official Mixer's Manual*, published in 1934. Duffy had worked in the Ashland House in New York, where the bar did a booming business during intermission at the nearby Lyceum Theater. Duffy was a bartender of the old school—the *very* old school, circa 1890. In his photo portrait at the front of the book, he looks out stiffly at the reader, attired in a heavy black suit and a derby hat. The philosophy is just as fusty. "I cannot too much deplore the custom which has become prevalent of late of free and general conversation between bartenders and patrons," Duffy wrote in his preface, sighing for the days when the men behind the bar knew their place and their trade, and starched white linen was mandatory (Duffy himself favored a red lapel carnation). His is the complaint of Jeeves in an era of blue jeans and rock music.

Not surprisingly, Duffy looked askance at the innovations of the Prohibition era. "Although we include in this collection many of the Cocktail Creations of those hectic days, we caution barkeepers and others against adopting some of them for general use." Indeed, Duffy marked with an asterisk those mixtures he disapproved of but felt it necessary to include "as a matter of record and as a mirror in which future Americans may see the follies which the enactment of the 18th Amendment produced."

On fundamentals, Duffy (who claims to have invented the highball in 1895) was a strict constructionist, insisting on a healthy respect for basic ingredients. He refused to countenance cocktails "which include Gin, Scotch, Brandy, Vermouth, and cream in one drink. Nor indeed, can we give our support to any concoction consisting of Gin and Rye, Gin and Scotch, Gin and Brandy, or to any beverage where two kinds of strong liquor are shaken together with bitters, cream, and Raspberry Syrup."

Fair enough, but Duffy's book reflects, perhaps more strikingly than any other drink book of the time, the changes wrought by fourteen years of Prohibition. Nearly half of his two hundred–odd pages devoted to cocktail recipes are taken up by gin-based drinks.

America never had enough time to recover from the ravages of

Prohibition and develop a new cocktail culture to replace the one that had been destroyed. Perhaps it never could have. The forces of modernization that swept over the country in the early twentieth century had rendered obsolete both the bartenders like Duffy and the elaborate establishments in which they worked. The cocktail of old had often been an overly complex, labor-intensive affair, as ornate and overstuffed as a Victorian parlor. The nineteenth-century bar books contain hundreds of recipes as extreme, demanding, and artificial as anything out of Escoffier. Changing circumstances demanded a streamlining of the cocktail, the kind of imaginative simplification that nouvelle cuisine brought to French cooking in our own time. Walter Dorwin Teague, the great industrial designer, appealed to the distillers to develop new packaging and bottle styles that would reflect the modern age.

But the sweep of events did not encourage the cocktail's evolution. If the hopped-up metabolism of prohibition dictated a period of slowdown, even somnolence, that was only to be expected. Advertisements tended to show their product enjoyed at leisure, in quiet, genteel settings. A highball at the nineteenth hole, perhaps, or in a library fitted out with a few discreet hunting trophies. The protagonist of the one-page magazine drama was generally a middle-aged or older man of substance—an insurance executive, say. With the nascent youth culture of the 1920s in full retreat, the idealized liquor consumer became a kind of mentor figure, wise in the ways of the world, demanding in matters of drink. Often he was surrounded by eager sycophants keen to show their enthusiasm for the old boy's favorite drink—inevitably a highball made with a "fine, aged whiskey" whose appreciation demanded a kind of apprenticeship.

The period of readjustment after Prohibition was made even more difficult by the fact that distillers had no stocks of liquor on hand, a particular hardship when it came to whiskey, which has to be aged. At the end of the 1934 fiscal year, 85 percent of the American whiskey inventory was less than a year old. Hence the emphasis on pedigree, which could take a preposterous turn. Mount Vernon rye, for example, claimed that it was first distilled "on the General's own estate," and that the whiskey was still made according to Washington's original recipe. All distillers favored dark-brown bottles whose nubbly, ornate surface patterns suggested a cut-glass decanter. The best defense is a good offense: If you're selling young whiskey, call it ancient.

No sooner had the situation begun to right itself than war broke out. By late 1942, all distillers were making "cocktails for Hitler": They shifted production to industrial alcohol, which went to make smokeless gunpowder and rubber tires. Except for three one-month "holidays" granted by the government, no new liquor was produced, except by a few rum and brandy facilities that could not easily be converted. Whiskey reserves plummeted.

More important, American men were now in uniform. Whatever its virtues, the military life does not promote appreciation of the fine points. Servicemen took what they could get when they could get it. "Military drinkers," wrote one newspaper columnist, "have been known to swallow anything from hair tonic to V-bomb juice to pernicious mixtures of Calvados-schnapps-champagne-red wine-brandy-cider-and-beer." In James Jones's *The Thin Red Line*, set in the South Pacific, C Company gets word that a field PX has been set up, with two items on offer: Barbasol shaving cream and Aqua Velva shaving lotion. The word spreads, and within hours the Aqua Velva disappears from the shelves and finds its way into cans of grapefruit juice: "It made a drink rather like a Tom Collins. Everybody loved it."

The Aqua Velva Collins was a sophisticate among improvised field cocktails. When aftershave or medical-supply alcohol could not be found, the inventive GI turned to local raw materials. The dried fruit that came with J and K rations could be soaked in water and transformed into jungle juice. A near cousin of jungle juice could be made by punching a hole in a coconut, adding a few teaspoons of sugar, plugging up the hole, and waiting several hours for the plug to blow out—an early-warning signal that the cocktail hour was nigh. The result tasted something like soap. In Polynesia and Melanesia, soldiers fermented the roots of the kava tree. "Night fighter" was the fermented sap of the nipa palm, and "tuba" was the fermented sap from the heart of a coconut tree—and so called because the sap was drawn off with a tube. On PT boats, sailors simply quaffed spare torpedo alcohol.

Stateside, taste bowed to necessity. With whiskey and gin hard to come by, America once again began exploring the margins, looking to Cuba, Puerto Rico, and Mexico. Between 1941 and 1944, consumption of rum increased fourfold, and for the first time, Americans became acquainted with a strange Mexican spirit called tequila. The quintessential forties cocktail was the Cuba Libre—rum and Coca-Cola—a harmless invention that was helped along by the Andrews Sisters song of the same name. The tune came from Trinidad, where some fifty thousand American servicemen ran a naval base—and were drinking a far better rum than the stuff unloaded on a captive American market.

With the end of the war, something like a return to normalcy set in—conservative normalcy. As part of a 1947 field report on U.S. drinking habits, *Life* magazine surveyed a Dallas club and found that 20 percent of the members were drinking beer, 33 percent highballs, 20 percent Manhattans or martinis, 13 percent whiskey sours, and 7 percent Tom Collinses. Solid, conservative, establishment drinks, reflecting straight-down-the-middle taste. That was to be the postwar order. No funny business, nothing suspicious or unsound.

The national taste was discovering the beauty of blandness. Blended whiskeys, lighter and less attractive, came to dominate the market. Initially, there was resistance. Immediately after Prohibition, the public regarded with a wary eye anything going under the name "blend"; the word had an unsavory meaning after the bootleggers' abuse. But the distillers, with limited stocks, pushed blended whiskey—essentially, good straight whiskey stretched out with neutral grain spirits—and won over the public.

In 1933, the head of Seagram's, the giant Canadian distiller, took a look south of the border and made a decision: the future lay in the lighter-bodied blended whiskeys. At the time, blends accounted for about 30 percent of the market. The company carried out exhaustive consumer surveys, sending its teams deep into the heart of straight-whiskey and bonded-whiskey territory. In one blind taste test after another, blends beat the straights and the bonded whiskeys 70 percent of the time. Seagram's considered the evidence and acted on it. The blends began to make dramatic headway, and with wartime conditions severely depleting whiskey stocks, they accounted for 90 percent of the market in 1946. As stocks of straight whiskey built up, the straights fought back, but they never gained more of a share than the taste tests suggested: somewhere between a quarter and a third of the market. By 1950, blends were outselling straights by eight to one.

The victory of blended whiskeys marks a turning point in American drinking taste and in the marketing of liquor. For the first time, the long-term trend, still dominant, toward lighter, less flavorful drinks was identified by the distillers and seized upon with a vengeance. It spelled an end to regional preferences as a serious factor in American drinking habits. As the major distillers consolidated into behemoths, they created and marketed national brands, least-common-denominator spirits geared to the mass taste.

By 1951, even *Business Week* felt compelled to comment on the blandness of the American palate. It noted with some alarm that advertising agencies were all promoting brands as "mild," "light," or "dry." Meanwhile, the top cocktails, in order, were the Scotch highball, the bourbon highball, and, just edging out the Manhattan, the martini.

Occasionally, creativity struck. But the more exotic cocktails of the period reflect a strange, synthetic exoticism. Take the Mai Tai. The drink was invented by Victor Bergeron—"Trader Vic"—who earned a niche in American popular culture with his Polynesian restaurants. According to the Trader himself, he first mixed the drink in 1944, at his Oakland restaurant, when he decided that the world needed another rum drink. "I took down a bottle of 17-year-old rum. It was J. Wray Nephew from Jamaica—surprisingly golden in color, medium-bodied, but with the rich pungent flavor particular to the Jamaican blends." He took fresh lime, curaçao, a dash of rock-candy syrup, and "a dollop of French orgeat for its subtle almond flavor." After shaking it up with ice, Vic poured it out for two friends visiting from Tahiti, who said, "Mai tai—roe aé," meaning "Out of this world—the best."

The enormous success of Trader Vic's restaurants remains one of the more fascinating chapters in American taste. It sheds light on a period that embraced blandness in food, drink, clothing, and even politics with a fervor that only fifteen hellish years of depression and war can account for. Shattered nerves ached for suburban lawns, easy-listening music, lots of air-conditioning, and predictability.

But man must have diversion of sorts. That's where Trader Vic came in. A native of Oakland, he opened a restaurant called Hinky

Dink's in the 1930s. The decor, heavy on the antlers and snowshoes, found favor with the public, and he prospered. His fondness for selling the decorations right off the wall gave him his nickname. On a trip to Los Angeles, Bergeron stumbled across a Polynesian restaurant called Don the Beachcomber, festooned with nets, floats, and other island paraphernalia. Bergeron raced back to Oakland and turned Hinky Dink's into a Polynesian fantasy. Out went the trophies, in came the South Sea masks, war clubs, and giant clamshells, with an Easter Island *moai* monolith out front for good measure.

Perhaps returning American servicemen found themselves growing nostalgic for the South Pacific. Perhaps the musical of the same name stirred a national longing to drink out of coconuts. Whatever the reason, Trader Vic's caught on and spread from city to city in the United States. Imitations were rife, and a healthy percentage of American restaurants seemed to be offering luaus and Hawaiian guitars. The concept and the execution were bogus, and Bergeron himself made no secret of it. "You can't eat real Polynesian food," he once said. "It's the most horrible junk I've ever tasted." So diners feasted on a thoroughly Americanized version of a less than compelling cuisine—and loved it. The drinks were about as authentic as the dishes: the White Witch, the Suffering Bastard, Dr. Funk of Tahiti, and Rangoon Ruby (vodka, lime, and cranberry juice, which resurfaced in the 1960s as the Bog Fog and now enjoys renown as the Cape Codder). The perfect accompaniment to Bongo Bongo Soup and Bah-Mee.

By the early 1960s, the tropical fad was humming along with enough velocity for Hawaii to begin marketing okolehao, a traditional firewater distilled from the root of the ti plant (the leaves can be seen on grass skirts). The cocktail chosen to launch this suspect beverage was Coke 'n' Oke. It did not catch on.

VODKA ÜBER ALLES

9

*"A small carafe of vodka,
very cold," ordered Bond.*

—Ian Fleming, Casino Royale (1953)

The fate of the cocktail after World War II can be read as a cold war allegory. The sanitized, commercialized version of middle-class life that defined the 1950s can be seen in the nation's drinking habits as well. The wayward creativity of the cocktail was tamed, a victim of social and political circumstances deeply hostile to eccentricity. The appetite for novelty that had launched a thousand drinks in the Gilded Age and the Roaring Twenties disappeared. The man in the gray flannel suit drank a dry martini, a gin and tonic, a Scotch and soda—safe choices that put you in solidly with the right people.

The fervor with which Americans pledged allegiance to the narrowest possible interpretation of the American way of life reflected a deep apprehension about the future and a bristling defensiveness in the face of the Communist threat. Here, too, the cocktail faithfully mirrors the political anguish of the time. At the precise moment when the United States was girding itself for an apocalyptic struggle with the Soviet Union and sharpening its vigilance against enemies within and without, the American way of drink was already succumbing to Russian influence. Its most cherished cocktails were being infiltrated—and falling, one by one, like so many dominoes—by vodka.

Today, the Eastern bloc has collapsed into dust, the two Germanys are one, the Soviet Union has disintegrated, and world Communism is beating a hasty, undignified retreat everywhere. Even Fidel looks shaky. But vodka has triumphed, utterly and completely.

For most Americans, vodka first flashed across the cultural screen at the Yalta and Teheran conferences, when the obligatory toasts were offered to Allied victory. FDR shook up a few of his wretched olive-brine martinis for Stalin and his aides. Unimpressed by this capitalist achievement, the Russians hoisted their traditional vodka, neat. It had warmed them in the desperate hours of Stalingrad's defense; it had propelled them across the ravaged Ukraine and onward to Europe and Berlin. This was no ordinary spirit.

Few Americans had ever heard of vodka. Those that had seemed to believe it came from potatoes, when in fact it is almost always distilled from grain. The first recipes calling for its use appear in the *Savoy Cocktail Book* (1930), which lists a Blue Monday (vodka, Cointreau, and blue vegetable juice) and a Russian Cocktail (crème de cacao, dry gin, and vodka: "shake well, strain into cocktail glass, and tossitoff quickski"). But the book was British and therefore unlikely to have been read by Americans; moreover, the United States did not recognize the Soviet Union until 1933, so imports of Russian vodka stood at zero. The odd bottle of Polish or Latvian vodka no doubt made its way to ethnic neighborhoods in the United States, but to all intents and purposes, the spirit was a mystery.

In 1934, however, a Russian émigré named Rudolph Kunett (né Kunetchansky) approached the sons of the Russian distiller Pierre Smirnoff and bought the American rights to his name and distilling process and set up operations in Bethel, Connecticut. Five years later, a Heublein executive, John G. Martin, paid fourteen thousand dollars and bought out the little distillery, which had been producing a grand total of twenty cases a day.

The customers, it so happened, were all out West. Like so many American enthusiasms, vodka began as a California phenomenon and then spread gradually to the rest of the country. Some clever marketing had a lot to do with it. Prompted by the "Smirnoff Leaves You Breathless" campaign, Americans discovered three convenient facts about vodka: it mixes with anything, it doesn't leave a heavy liquor taste or smell, and it looks light and clean, even dietetic. Folk wisdom had it that vodka would not inflict a hangover. It also had a cocktail gimmick behind it. In 1946, John Martin of Heublein ran into a friend who owned a Los Angeles restaurant called the Cock 'n' Bull. The restaurateur, who was British, had been trying to push imported ginger beer at his bar, with no success. Martin saw an opportunity to promote his vodka. The result was the Moscow Mule: vodka, ginger beer, and half a lime, served in a copper mug.

For the first time, an invented cocktail was being used as a marketing device. "The Moscow Mule was a Trojan horse," said the adman who steered Smirnoff's campaign. "It introduced vodka to the American people." Heublein salesmen traveled from bar to bar, explaining the drink to bar managers and bartenders and supplying "Moscow Mule" signs to be displayed on walls and mirrors. Legend has it that in 1947, Joan Crawford threw a party and decreed that only vodka and champagne should be served. Her guests found the new drink chic and began serving it at their parties too. Less glamorously, it has been theorized that the film community latched onto vodka because it allowed them to drink on the set and still elude the sharp eyes (and nostrils) of the studio spies.

Vodka was on its way. Slowly but inexorably it spread from Los Angeles to San Diego and San Francisco, and then rolled eastward. "From a potable *rara avis*, in the same class as usquebaugh and arrack," the *New York Times* said in 1947, "it has become standard equipment in bars and cocktail lounges throughout the country." Indeed, the Oak Room Bar at the Plaza Hotel was up to the minute, serving a Volga (vodka with orange juice, lemon juice, and grenadine). The real growth lay ahead, however. Vodka had made a ripple, not a wave. At least, not until the early 1950s.

Then vodka began to take off. From perhaps 40,000 cases in 1950, sales leaped to 1.1 million cases in 1954, then increased fourfold the following year, when the word "vodkatini" entered the language. In 1967, vodka overtook gin; nine years later, it surpassed whiskey, to become the leading spirit consumed in the United States. And so it remains today. Game, set, and match to the Russians.

Even the Soviet Union's archenemy James Bond drank vodka. In his lethal hands, vodka seemed less a drink than a bracing tonic, not unlike the high-velocity showers that washed away, in a matter of minutes, the effects of a SMERSH-administered beating. Like Bond himself, vodka was lean, clean, antiseptic, astringent, the appropriate fuel for a finely tuned engine of death.

Ironically, even as the Russians were dominating the cocktail abroad, at home they were inflicting on themselves a series of humiliating defeats. The same nation that had developed the hydrogen bomb and beaten the Americans into outer space could not create a drinkable cocktail. In 1954, with great fanfare, the Cocktail Hall opened its doors on Gorky Street in Moscow. Within, the management presented the state of the art in Communist mixology, the proletarian response to such capitalist icons as the martini and the Manhattan. Only a Soviet fashion house could have created anything more appalling. The Cocktail Hall proved beyond a doubt that only in a free society can the mixed drink thrive. Tops on the menu was something called the Battering Ram: vodka and Armenian brandy, to which a depth charge of peach, plum, and apricot brandies was added. The Lighthouse was sweet "hunter's vodka," port, and a teaspoon of cherry jam, while the Health Resort called for Georgian brandy, Chartreuse, madeira, and Soviet champagne, with a garnish of two dried prunes.

Yet, in the end, vodka has contributed very little to the cocktail. Insidiously, it has slipped in and offered itself as a tasteless substitute for gin. The gin and tonic became the vodka tonic. The orange blossom became the screwdriver. Only old-timers remember that the gimlet was once a gin drink. And sometime in the 1970s, the martini—yes, the martini—became a vodka drink for most Americans.

As the classics underwent a vodka conversion, the rising generation discovered that vodka served its purposes ideally. Dead set against the old-fashioned discipline known as acquired taste, the youth of America embraced vodka unreservedly. Here was a miraculous thing: an alcoholic beverage that was, by legal definition, "without distinctive character, aroma, or taste." With vodka, the cocktail shed all its complications overnight, becoming nothing more than a goosed-up fruit drink—Hawaiian Punch with some zing to it.

Vodka has given us the Bloody Mary, no small achievement. Oddly enough, the drink's origins are nearly as difficult to tease out as the martini's. The comedian George Jessel took credit for its invention, but Fernand Petiot, a bartender at Harry's New York Bar in Paris in the 1920s, who made his way to the St. Regis Hotel in New York, claimed in 1964 that Jessel's Bloody Mary was nothing more than vodka and tomato juice. Petiot's creation, originally called a Red Snapper, added Worcestershire sauce, lemon juice, salt and cayenne pepper, and a celery stick.

Like a two-stage rocket, vodka continues to climb. The budget and midpriced brands have more or less plateaued in recent years, but the so-called superpremium vodkas—the high-priced imports—soar ever upward, powered by some very shrewd marketing and image doctoring. In the 1970s, Stolichnaya from the Soviet Union established the fact that richer consumers will pay more for the prestige of an import. This golden truth, familiar to the auto industry for some time and to the luxury trade for centuries, revolutionized the liquor industry. The big money was to be made at the top end of the market, where volumes were small but the profit margins nice and fat.

"Stoly on the rocks" became a status statement at bars across the land. Then the Soviets shot down Korean Airlines flight 007. Overnight, Stoly became a target of hatred. Seizing the opportunity, Absolut vodka, from peace-loving, neutral Sweden, launched a major marketing campaign to win the Stoly customer, a campaign so successful that it ended up redefining the image of vodka.

Absolut used its ads to make a style statement. The campaign, still going strong, presents visual and verbal puns based on the Absolut name. In the early days, artists like Andy Warhol and Keith Haring were enlisted to design ads with minimal text—"Absolut Warhol" and "Absolut Haring." An "Absolut Christmas" ad turned the Absolut bottle into a snow scene, manufactured so that magazine readers could turn the page upside down and set snowflakes in motion.

With its precision-engineered name and minimalist bottle, Absolut embodied the myth of purity that is central to vodka's current appeal. The old Smirnoff "breathless" campaigns more or less came out and announced, "Look, we all want a drink at midday, but it's starting to look bad." Absolut never so much as hinted that the product was actually alcoholic. It made a compelling design statement, with a bottle that looked like a fireplug designed by Mies van der Rohe. The name implied that here at last could be found vodka from which the final traces of imperfection had been purged. The product could go on the shelf next to the designer spring waters and look right at home. With Absolut, the age of the healthy cocktail has begun.

POSTSCRIPT

The triumph of vodka sends a disquieting signal. It represents taste cut adrift from its moorings, floating aimlessly on a bland, tepid sea. Vodka itself is not to blame. In the great republic of drink (to shift the metaphor), it has an honorable role to play; but it threatens to assume dictatorial powers. Moreover, it has risen to its present exalted state for all the wrong reasons. It stands as a symbol of post-Prohibition drinking in America, which has been a dreary saga of industry consolidation, mass marketing of image, and anxious trend-watching.

The cocktail has suffered as a result. In the past, when liquor companies were small and advertising had not yet begun to dream of mass persuasion, the cocktail's laboratory of invention was the local bar. Its chief scientist was the fellow with the handlebar mustache standing behind the mahogany, its consumer and judge the man with his foot on the brass rail. Today, the inspiration for cocktails tends to come from liquor companies keen on boosting sales of a particular product.

In principle, there's nothing wrong with industry-generated recipes. Who knows the product and its potential better, after all? It makes sense that the distiller *should* create the best cocktails. But let us judge the results. In 1951, for example, Seagram's tried to boost sales of its Ancient Golden gin with a gin-and-grapefruit-juice cocktail it dubbed the Seabreeze. It failed. In 1960, the producers of Galliano liqueur launched something called the Golden Dream, with equally dismal results. Undeterred, Galliano struck again in 1970 with the Harvey Wallbanger—orange juice, vodka, and a dash of Galliano. This time, the company backed the cocktail with a major advertising campaign that featured a jolly little cartoon character named Harvey. The approach paid off. Sales of Galliano tripled in three years.

But the drinks survived only as long as advertising supported them. Precisely the same phenomenon can be observed in the extraordinary peach schnapps bonanza of the mid-1980s, and a cocktail called the Fuzzy Navel. Peach schnapps was developed by a flavor scientist named Earl LaRoe, working for National Distillers, subsequently bought out by DeKuyper. Back in the early 1980s, he and his colleagues at the flavor lab were hot on the trail of what LaRoe, now retired, calls "the big, fresh-peach profile," with an eye to creating something exciting in the schnapps line. LaRoe remains secretive about his discovery, but the results are unignorably public. With virtually no advertising, Peachtree Schnapps caught on and became the first spirit since repeal to sell more than a million cases in its first year. Before long, forty different brands of peach schnapps were on the market. In Iowa, peach schnapps outsold all other spirits.

This was a fad bordering on a frenzy. And at the center of it was an idiotic-sounding cocktail called the Fuzzy Navel. In the Midwest particularly, where schnapps had always been popular, the Fuzzy Navel and its even sillier relatives—the Silk Panties (peach schnapps and Stolichnaya vodka), the Slippery Nipple, and, most embarrassingly of all, the Teeny Weeny Woo Woo (peach schnapps, vodka, and cranberry juice)—became a kind of cult, a rallying point for young drinkers in search of fun and not too picky about taste. Eager to cash in, the distillers released a tidal wave of flavored schnapps in the ensuing years: pear, strawberry, even root beer. Alas, the sort of customer who could step up to the bar with a straight face and demand a Teeny Weeny Woo Woo proved to be unreliable. Flavored schnapps enjoyed its fifteen minutes of fame, and then American youth, wearied, stampeded to the next attraction with a risqué ring to it. It's the nightclub syndrome: The hot spot that has to position storm troopers at the entrance one week finds itself a pathetic supplicant the next, pressing free passes into the palms of a now indifferent public.

The schnapps audience quickly embraced such delights as the Screaming Orgasm (Grand Marnier, Kahlúa, and Bailey's Irish Cream) or the aforementioned Jell-O Shot, whose consumption, from a little paper cup, is elegantly known as "sucking slime." A Houston magazine reports that local cosmopolitans now enjoy something called a Lava Lamp: vodka and soda with chunks of Jell-O floating in it.

This downward slide threatens to take the bartender with it. If the cocktail comes to be nothing more than a fashion accent with a funny name, the job requirement for bartenders will quickly follow suit. They may be phased out altogether. A company called Honeybee Robotics has created Robotender, a mechanical barman with a video monitor for a head. It can shake up more than a hundred different drinks. It can tell jokes. It can tune itself out and show music videos.

Is the cocktail doomed? In the eighteenth century, literary critics, looking anxiously at the poetry of their own age, began an extended debate that has become known as the quarrel between the ancients and the moderns. The central issue was this: Had the Greeks and Romans exhausted the richest veins of literary material, leaving only scattered pockets of ore for later generations to mine? Were modern writers, as Samuel Johnson put it, "the moons of literature," shining with a light reflected from the ancients?

The cocktail finds itself in an analogous position. After the golden age of the late nineteenth century, and the silver age of Prohibition, America has entered an age of brass. And the traditional sources of inspiration appear to be drying up. The corner bar has entered into decline. The Happy Hour no longer spreads the sound of laughter throughout the land. Bartending, once a proud profession, is now a pit stop between acting jobs or, if the Hollywood bomb *Cocktail* can be believed, an opportunity for picking up women and learning how to juggle shakers like Indian clubs. The possibility that we will ever again see new cocktails with the classic virtues of the martini or the Manhattan seems remote.

But wait. Two signs of hope appear on the horizon: immigrants and yuppies. In the past, the trail of conquest (or, more often, a shortage of raw materials) has led Americans to the geographic margins. That's how rum and tequila first made their way across the border and into cocktail glasses, opening up new potentials for the cocktail that have yet to be fully exploited. The WASP, patrician era of the cocktail may be exhausted, but America stands on the threshold of exciting multicultural developments. The third world could well impart new vigor to the first, as it has in popular music. Already the great rums of the Caribbean have contributed genuine classics to the cocktail repertoire. On the Parnassus of drink, the daiquiri strolls arm in arm with the martini, both attired in toga and laurels. In our own century, the bars of San Juan, Puerto Rico, yielded the piña colada: at 104 Fortaleza Street, site of the former Barrachina Bar, a bronze plaque honors the memory of Don Ramón Portas Mingot, who in 1963 began whipping crushed ice, sweet cream, coconut cream, fresh pineapple juice, and rum in a blender. (The achievement is contested by Ramón

Marrero Pérez, known as Poppa Monchito, of the Caribe Hilton, who says he created the piña colada in 1954.) Sometime in the 1930s, Mexico brought forth the margarita, which, despite a devaluation in the form of frozen-fruit margaritas, ranks very near the top of any classic cocktail list.

The tropical cocktail represents an attitude toward leisure and drink that seems to encourage creativity in the cocktail line. Americans go to the Caribbean and Mexico primed for difference. The old drinks won't do. They look forward to something surprising in the glass, and local bars work hard to deliver. Ingredients are fresh and local. This happy set of circumstances comes near to reproducing the great cocktail age of the 1880s and 1890s, when the premium was on novelty, ingenuity, and display.

Rum and tequila promise great things for the future. And this is where that much maligned species the yuppie comes in. Is it too late to say a word for America's young upwardly mobile urban professionals? Their reign was brief and often obnoxious, but in a number of key sectors, America owes a debt to them. The country eats better today because of the yuppies. It's now reasonable to expect at least one decent restaurant even in a small town, a little sanctuary where the wine list offers something besides a lethally chilled bottle of hearty burgundy. The local tavern is likely to offer something more tantalizing than a shot of blended whiskey and a watery beer.

One school of thought insists that the purpose of a bar is to dispense a shot and a beer, keep the lighting low, and skip the pretentious nonsense. The workingman needs no ferns. But in this matter, as in so many others, the workingman has been sold a bill of goods. The constriction of choice that set in after Prohibition was un-American, an assault on core values as ruthless in its own way as the forced collectivization of agriculture in the USSR. The malign forces of modernization conspired to homogenize—to blandify—the American diet. Only awesome, sustained pressure could have convinced the citizenry of a free country that it liked the aerated, tasteless dough product known as white bread, a deep and abiding mystery to immigrants. Only sensory deprivation can account for a relatively well-to-do couple, like Tom and Betsy Rath, in *The Man in the Gray Flannel Suit*, planning a big splurge meal consisting of sparkling burgundy and a big steak.

As with food, so with drink: the distinctive regional bourbons, ryes, and beers disappeared one by one. The inventive spirit that had sustained the cocktail flagged in the face of national apathy and a dogged allegiance to perhaps two or three standard drinks. This is the dismal state of affairs that for decades has been regarded as the natural condition of drink in America. Like meat loaf, institutionalized blandness has been with us long enough to be regarded as a kind of tradition. Tampering with the basics seems unpatriotic. Fortunately, the children of the 1960s were not content to let things rest.

Fussy and particular, the yuppie turned out to have a whim of iron. He simply *would* not, *could* not, bring anything but an imported beer to his lips, or the rarest of single-malt Scotches. In cocktails as in food, he insisted on authenticity, integrity of ingredients, and top quality all the way around. For this let us give thanks, even if snobbery and status seeking often lay behind the ruthless "pursuit of excellence," even if there is something a bit self-conscious and twee—postmodern, in fact—about stepping up to the bar and ordering a sidecar or a Jack Rose. But sometimes snobbery has its uses. The image-conscious drinker who insists on the best as a form of self-advertisement winds up as often as not educating his taste buds and, in the end, actually learning how to discriminate between good, better, and best. Somewhere along the way, the snob develops respect for the subject matter, whether it's wines of the Loire, English bitters, or single-malt Scotches. Arrogance gives way to humility, image-mongering to the disinterested pursuit of knowledge. This is the yuppie way of knowing, the seven upscale pillars of wisdom. Heap scorn if you will, but America and the cocktail are the better for it.

RECIPES

The 110 recipes in this section reflect my own biases and taste. I have tried to provide a reasonably equal distribution among the various spirit groups and to include classics, worthy but forgotten cocktails of the past, and promising newcomers. If the list seems heavy on the champagne cocktails, that's because they kick off a social occasion with great flair, and most hosts are more willing to concoct fancy cocktails at the beginning of the evening than at the end. Rye whiskey also pops up more often than its popularity might seem to warrant. But most of the whiskey cocktails of the golden age were designed with rye in mind, and the present age, which places a premium on dryness, should be delighted to rediscover the great whiskey of the East. Three companies make a straight rye today: Old Overholt (my choice), Wild Turkey, and Jim Beam. The list includes six nonalcoholic cocktails, which come in handy for guests who do not drink or who are acting as designated driver for the evening. There's no reason why nondrinkers can't enjoy something with a bit of flavor to it.

The reader should note with some relief that only a modest bar is required to make the cocktails on the list. Anyone starting from scratch can work up to fighting strength by buying a bottle each of bourbon, straight rye, Scotch, light and amber rum, a modest cognac, gin, applejack, vodka, sweet and dry vermouth, tequila, Campari, Angostura bitters, Cointreau, tonic, and soda. Stick to high-quality spirits. The better the materials, the better the drink. The hardware should include a cocktail shaker, a cocktail strainer, a long-handled stirrer, and a jigger (actually, two metal measuring cups joined at the bottom, the larger one measuring an ounce and a half and known as a jigger, the smaller one measuring an ounce and known as a pony). Since fruit juices should be squeezed from fresh fruit (no mixes, no concentrates), a sturdy manual juicer is a good idea, although the bare hand works fine. Mechanical juicers tend to throw pulp and rind into the drink. When a cocktail requires a twist of the rind, use a razor-sharp potato peeler—Kuhn Rika from Switzerland is perfect. The idea is to create an oil-filled sliver of outer rind, with no trace of the bitter white inner rind. Ambitious mixers might try squeezing the twist over a lit match held about six inches above the drink. The volatile oil from the skin will ignite in spectacular fashion and distribute a pleasing, delicate slick of burnt lemon, lime, or orange over the drink surface. You'll need a thicker layer of fruit skin to do this.

Too much psychic distress has been caused by the shake-versus-stir controversy. Liquors do not bruise, so there's no point in being squeamish. But shaking will ruin an effervescent drink—that is, one containing champagne, soda, or tonic. And it will overly aerate tomato juice. Those exceptions aside, anything else can be shaken, the best method of getting a cocktail as cold as possible as quickly as possible (crushed or cracked ice is ideal).

But what then? If you strain the drink into a glass, it sits there without ice and will return to room temperature before long. Strain it over ice, and you have a drink that stays cold longer but eventually becomes an insipid soup. And remember, there has already been some dilution from melting in the shaker. It's a classic trade-off. I prefer to keep the flavors concentrated and properly balanced, so I shake and strain, and have so indicated in the directions to the drinks in this section. But this is purely a personal matter.

Finally, every bar should have a bottle of simple syrup for sweetening drinks. Granulated sugar tends to settle to the bottom of the glass, while simple syrup blends perfectly with any drink. To make simple syrup, heat equal parts sugar and water (say, two cups each) in a saucepan until the sugar dissolves. Pour the solution into a bottle or decanter, preferably one with a narrow metal pouring spout attached to a cork. The syrup will keep indefinitely. The recipes below assume the use of granulated sugar. One teaspoon sugar equals two dashes of sugar syrup.

Drinks marked with an asterisk are discussed in some detail in the text.

WHISKEY COCKTAILS

POLICE GAZETTE COCKTAIL

From the *Police Gazette Bartenders Guide* (1901)

3 ounces whiskey
3 dashes simple syrup
2 dashes Angostura bitters
2 dashes curaçao
2 dashes maraschino
2 dashes French vermouth
1 maraschino cherry

Mix liquid ingredients with cracked ice, serve in cocktail glass with cherry.

SAZERAC *

In his *Famous New Orleans Drinks* (1940), Stanley Clisby Arthur gives the following recipe, as mixed by Leon Dupont, a former bartender at the Sazerac House. Most modern recipes call for bourbon instead of rye, and only one bitters, Peychaud's. Herbsaint is a New Orleans substitute for absinthe.

1 cube sugar
3 drops Peychaud's bitters
Dash Angostura bitters
1½ ounces straight rye
Dash absinthe substitute
  (Pernod, Ricard, or
  Herbsaint)
Twist of lemon

Fill an old-fashioned glass with cracked ice and let chill. In a second old-fashioned glass place a cube of sugar and add just enough water to moisten. Crush the saturated sugar with a bar spoon. Add a few drops Peychaud's bitters, a dash of Angostura, and rye. Add several lumps of ice and stir. Empty first glass of its ice, add several drops of Pernod, Ricard, or Herbsaint; twirl the glass to coat the sides, and pour out any excess liquid. Into this glass strain the whiskey mixture, then twist a piece of lemon peel over it.

MINT JULEP *

1 teaspoon superfine sugar
4 sprigs mint
3 ounces bourbon

Fill a collins glass with crushed ice. In a small glass, muddle the sugar and the leaves from two mint sprigs with a dash of water. Add the bourbon, stir, and strain into the collins glass. Stir until the glass frosts. Garnish with the remaining mint sprigs.

MINT JULEP À LA CREOLE

From the *Original Picayune Cookbook* (1901)

1 cup water
6 sprigs fresh young mint
3 cubes sugar
1 tablespoon brandy or
  whiskey
Lemon or orange peel
Juice of ½ lemon
A few ripe strawberries

Take one large cut glass, half filled with water, add mint sprigs and sugar cubes, and stir well until the sugar is absorbed. Add brandy or whiskey and stir. Add lemon or orange peel and lemon juice. Fill the glass with crushed ice and decorate top with mint sprigs. Place a few ripe strawberries on top of the mint, and sprinkle lightly with sugar.

OLD-FASHIONED *

The invention of the old-fashioned—an abbreviated name for "old-fashioned whiskey cocktail"—has often been credited to the Pendennis Club of Louisville, Kentucky. Legend has it that Colonel James E. Pepper, a noted bourbon distiller, brought the recipe East when he traveled on business. The actual facts remain to be discovered. There is no question, though, that the old-fashioned is one of the oldest and best cocktails.

1 cube sugar
Dash Angostura bitters
2 to 3 ounces bourbon
Twist of lemon

Muddle a sugar cube in the bottom of old-fashioned glass with a few drops of water and a dash of Angostura bitters. Add bourbon and ice cubes, garnish with a twist of lemon.

MANHATTAN *

1 ½ ounces straight rye
(preferably) or
bourbon
¼ ounce sweet vermouth
¼ ounce dry vermouth
Dash Angostura bitters
Maraschino cherry for
garnish (optional)

Pour liquid ingredients into an ice-filled shaker. Shake, then strain into cocktail glass; garnish with a maraschino cherry (optional).

REMSEN COOLER

The name comes from a now extinct brand of whiskey.

½ teaspoon superfine sugar
4 ounces club soda
2 to 3 ounces Scotch or gin
Twist of lemon

Dissolve sugar in a splash of club soda in a collins glass. Add ice, Scotch (or gin), and stir. Top with club soda and serve with a twist of lemon.

WHISKEY COLLINS

2 ounces straight rye or
bourbon
Juice of ½ lemon
1 teaspoon powdered sugar
4 ounces club soda

Pour rye (or bourbon), lemon juice, and sugar into an ice-filled collins glass, fill with soda, and stir.

A L G O N Q U I N

2 ounces straight rye
I ounce dry vermouth
I ounce pineapple juice

Pour ingredients into an ice-filled shaker. Shake, then strain into a cocktail glass.

R O B   R O Y

I ½ ounces Scotch
I ½ ounces sweet vermouth
2 dashes Angostura bitters
Twist of lemon

Pour liquid ingredients into an ice-filled shaker. Shake, then strain into a cocktail glass. Garnish with a twist of lemon.

W A R D   8 *

I ½ ounces straight rye
    or bourbon
½ ounce orange juice
½ ounce lemon juice
3 dashes grenadine

Pour ingredients into an ice-filled shaker. Shake, then strain into a cocktail glass.

WHISKEY SOUR

1 ½ ounces rye or bourbon
½ ounce lemon juice
½ ounce lime juice
1 teaspoon powdered sugar

Pour ingredients into an ice-filled shaker. Shake, then strain into a cocktail glass.

BROOKLYN

From *The Official Mixer's Manual* (1934), by Patrick Gavin Duffy

2 ounces straight rye
1 ounce dry vermouth
Dash Amer Picon
Dash maraschino

Pour ingredients into an ice-filled shaker. Shake, then strain into a cocktail glass.

ROYAL

From Lafcadio Hearn's *La Cuisine Créole* (1885)

3 ounces whiskey or brandy
2 tablespoons ginger beer
1 teaspoon sugar
Dash Angostura bitters
Twist of lemon

Pour all ingredients except lemon into an ice-filled shaker. Shake, then strain into a cocktail glass and garnish with a twist of lemon.

NEW YORKER

From *The Stork Club Bar Book* (1946)

2 ounces straight rye
Juice of ½ lime
Dash grenadine
Twist of lemon

Pour liquid ingredients into an ice-filled shaker. Shake, then strain into a cocktail glass. Serve with a twist of lemon.

AFFINITY

2 ounces Scotch
½ ounce sweet vermouth
½ ounce dry vermouth
2 to 3 dashes Angostura bitters

Pour ingredients into an ice-filled shaker. Shake, then strain into a cocktail glass.

APPROVE

From *The Savoy Cocktail Book* (1930)

3 ounces straight rye
2 dashes Angostura bitters
2 dashes Cointreau
Lemon and orange peel

Pour liquid ingredients into an ice-filled shaker. Shake, then strain into a cocktail glass. Squeeze lemon and orange peel on top.

LEMON PUNCH

From *National Cookery Book* (1826)

12 lemons
2 pounds loaf sugar
1 quart whiskey

Roll 12 lemons and pare off the yellow rind very thin. Boil the rinds in a gallon of water until the flavor is extracted. Strain the liquid and discard the rinds. Squeeze lemons over 2 pounds of loaf sugar and add them to the lemon water. Stir in 1 quart whiskey and bottle the punch.

BARBARY COAST

From G. Selmer Fougner's "Along the Wine Trail" column, *New York Sun* (1934)

2 ounces straight rye
½ ounce dry vermouth
½ ounce orange juice

Pour ingredients into an ice-filled shaker. Shake, then strain into a cocktail glass.

BRANDY COCKTAILS

NICKY FINN

This 1946 recipe came from Nicky Quattrociocchi, owner of El Borracho restaurant in New York.

1 ounce brandy
1 ounce Cointreau
1 ounce lemon juice
Dash Pernod

Pour ingredients into an ice-filled shaker. Shake, then strain into a cocktail glass.

SIDECAR

The one classic cocktail to emerge from Prohibition. Harry's New York Bar in Paris claims the honor of inventing it, in 1931. But it flows freely in Carl Van Vechten's 1930 short story collection, *Parties,* while David A. Embury, author of *The Fine Art of Mixing Drinks* (1948), says the drink was invented by a friend of his shortly after World War I and named after the sidecar in which the friend traveled to his favorite Paris bistro. Inexplicably, *The American Mercury* in 1933 refers to it as "a ladies' drink," which is absurd.

1 ounce brandy or cognac
Juice of ½ lemon (or ½ lime)
½ ounce Cointreau

Pour ingredients into an ice-filled shaker. Shake, then strain into a cocktail glass.

JACK ROSE

Jack Rose was a gangster who turned state's evidence in the notorious gangland slaying of Herman Rosenthal, a gambling-house operator, near Times Square in 1912. But common sense suggests that the name combines the base spirit (applejack) and the color of the drink.

1½ ounces applejack
Juice of 1 lime
½ ounce grenadine

Pour ingredients into an ice-filled shaker. Shake, then strain into a cocktail glass.

ARMAGNAC LILLI

1 ounce Armagnac
4 ounces blond Lillet
Orange twist or wedge

Pour Armagnac and Lillet over shaved ice in champagne flute. Garnish with orange.

CALVADOS COCKTAIL

2 ounces calvados
2 ounces orange juice
Dash Cointreau
Twist of orange peel

Pour liquid ingredients into an ice-filled shaker. Shake, then strain into a cocktail glass, and serve with a twist of orange peel.

STAR

Supposedly created at the Plaza Hotel in New York in 1911, it was famous enough by the teens to be celebrated by Franklin P. Adams in his "Conning Tower" column for the *New York Sun.*

1½ ounces applejack
1½ ounces sweet vermouth

Pour the applejack and vermouth into an ice-filled shaker. Shake, then strain into a glass.

POUSSE L'AMOUR

1 ounce Armagnac
½ ounce orange juice
3 drops Cointreau
4 ounces champagne
Orange slice

Prechill the Armagnac and orange juice. Pour into a champagne flute, add Cointreau, and top up with champagne. Garnish with an orange slice.

GIN DRINKS

AVIATION

From *The Savoy Cocktail Book* (1930)

2 ounces gin
1 ounce lemon juice
2 dashes maraschino

Pour ingredients into an ice-filled shaker and strain into a cocktail glass.

GIN DAISY

2 ounces gin
Juice of ½ lemon
½ teaspoon powdered sugar
1 teaspoon raspberry syrup
  or grenadine

Pour ingredients into an ice-filled shaker. Shake, then strain into a cocktail glass.

GIN BUCK

Juice of ¼ lemon
3 ounces gin
4 ounces ginger ale

Squeeze lemon into a highball glass, add cracked ice and gin. Stir and fill with ginger ale.

STORK CLUB

From *The Stork Club Cocktail Book* (1946)

1½ ounces gin
Juice of ½ orange
Dash lime juice
Dash Cointreau
Dash Angostura bitters

Pour ingredients into an ice-filled shaker. Shake, then pour into a cocktail glass.

ABBEY

2 ounces gin
1 ounce orange juice
1 ounce blond Lillet
Dash Angostura bitters
Maraschino cherry

Pour liquid ingredients into an ice-filled shaker. Shake, then strain into a cocktail glass. Add a maraschino cherry.

PERFECT

An early classic, served at the old Waldorf bar in the 1890s.

1½ ounces gin
1 ounce sweet vermouth
1 ounce dry vermouth
Dash Angostura bitters
Orange peel

Pour gin and vermouths into an ice-filled shaker. Shake, then strain into a cocktail glass. Add a dash of bitters and a twist of orange.

THE FLAME OF LOVE

Courtesy Chasen's Restaurant, Hollywood

Scant teaspoon dry (fino)
    sherry
Orange peel
1–2 ounces gin or vodka

In a chilled martini glass, swirl the sherry to coat the sides, and pour out any excess. Pass a thick slab of orange peel over the flame of a lit match, squeezing the peel. The oil contained in the peel should ignite and deposit a fine burnt-orange spray over the surface of the glass. Discard peel. Fill glass with ice and add an ounce or two of gin or vodka. Twirl repeatedly with bar spoon. Repeat orange-peel ignition, discarding peel. Serve.

CAMPDEN

2 ounces gin
1 ounce Cointreau
1 ounce blond Lillet

Pour ingredients into an ice-filled shaker. Shake, then strain into a cocktail glass.

BRONX *

1½ ounces gin
½ ounce sweet vermouth
½ ounce dry vermouth
Juice of ¼ orange

Pour ingredients into an ice-filled shaker. Shake, then strain into a cocktail glass.

VESPER (JAMES BOND MARTINI)

3 ounces gin
I ounce vodka
½ ounce blond Lillet
Lemon peel

Named after Vesper Lynd, the doomed love interest in *Casino Royale*. "I never have more than one drink before dinner," said Bond. "But I do like that one to be very large and very strong and very cold and very well made."

Pour liquid ingredients into an ice-filled shaker, shake, and strain into a martini glass. Add a large, thin slice of lemon peel.

MARTINI *

3 ounces gin or vodka
Dry vermouth to taste
Garnish to taste

In an ice-filled shaker, pour ingredients in a ratio of five to one for a dry martini, as little as a drop or two of vermouth for an extra-dry. Shake, then strain into a martini glass. Garnish with a lemon twist or an olive. A garnish of a cocktail onion makes the drink a Gibson.

FRENCH 75

The name refers to a French gun in World War I.

I ½ ounces gin
Juice of ½ lemon
½ teaspoon powdered sugar
4 ounces champagne
Twist of lemon

Mix the gin, lemon juice, and sugar in a collins glass half filled with crushed ice. Top up with chilled champagne, and add a twist of lemon.

RAMOS GIN FIZZ[*]

1½ ounces gin
1 tablespoon powdered
  sugar
3–4 drops orange-flower
  water
Juice of ½ lime
Juice of ½ lemon
1 egg white
1½ ounces cream
1 squirt seltzer
2 drops vanilla extract
  (optional)

Mix ingredients in a tall bar glass in the order given. Add crushed ice, not too fine, since lumps help froth the egg white. Shake for a good long time, until mixture acquires body. Strain into a tall, thin glass.

QUATORZE

Courtesy Quatorze Restaurant, New York

3 ounces gin
1 ounce blond Lillet
Splash Noyau de Poissy
Orange peel

Pour liquid ingredients into a shaker. Shake, then strain into a chilled cocktail glass. Serve with a twist of orange peel.

CITY BREEZE

Courtesy City Restaurant, Los Angeles

2 ounces Pimm's
3 ounces Lemon Ginger Tea
  (recipe follows)
I ounce gin float
Sprig of mint
Slice of lemon and lime

Pour Pimm's, 3 ounces strained lemon ginger tea, and gin float into a pitcher of ice. Stir. Garnish with mint and lemon and lime slices.

Lemon Ginger Tea

I quart water
Juice of I lemon
¼ cup freshly grated ginger
¼ cup honey

Bring the water to a boil. Add the lemon juice, the squeezed lemon, and the ginger. Let steep about 20 minutes. Stir in honey, strain. Can be used to make the City Breeze or served as a nonalcoholic drink over ice with thin slices of lemon and lime, or hot with cinnamon sticks.

NEGRONI

2 ounces gin
I ounce Campari
I ounce sweet vermouth
Orange slice

Pour gin, Campari, and vermouth over ice cubes in a short glass. Garnish with an orange slice.

TOM COLLINS

2 ounces gin
Juice of ½ lemon
1 teaspoon powdered sugar
Club soda
Lemon or orange slice

Pour gin, lemon juice, and sugar into a tall glass filled with ice, top up with soda, and garnish with a slice of lemon or orange.

SHADY GROVE COOLER

2 ounces gin
Juice of ½ lemon
½ tablespoon sugar
4 to 5 ounces ginger beer

Pour gin and lemon juice into a tall glass filled with ice. Add sugar and stir. Top up with ginger beer.

SOUTH SIDE FIZZ

2 ounces gin
Juice of ½ lemon
Club soda
Sprig of mint

Pour gin and lemon juice into a tall glass filled with ice. Top up with soda. Garnish with mint.

GIN FIZZ

1 ½ ounces gin
1 ounce lemon juice
1 teaspoon fine granulated
  sugar
Club soda

Pour gin, lemon juice, and sugar into an ice-filled shaker. Shake, then strain into a 10-ounce highball glass. Top up with soda and stir slightly.

HOFFMAN HOUSE FIZZ

3 ounces gin
Juice of ½ lemon
½ tablespoon powdered sugar
2 dashes maraschino
Juice of ¼ orange
1 teaspoon grenadine
4 ounces club soda

Pour all ingredients but club soda into an ice-filled shaker. Shake, then strain into a highball glass and top up with soda.

BARON

2 ounces gin
1 ounce dry vermouth
6 dashes curaçao
2 dashes sweet vermouth
Twist of lemon

Pour liquid ingredients into an ice-filled shaker. Shake, then strain into a cocktail glass. Add a twist of lemon.

BEAUTY SPOT

2 ounces gin
1 ounce grenadine
White of 1 egg

Pour ingredients into an ice-filled shaker. Shake, then strain into a cocktail glass.

BRONX TERRACE

2 ounces gin
1 ounce dry vermouth
Juice of ½ lime
Maraschino cherry

Pour liquid ingredients into an ice-filled shaker. Shake, then strain into a cocktail glass. Add a maraschino cherry.

DEPTH CHARGE

2 ounces gin
2 ounces blond Lillet
2 dashes Ricard or Pernod
Orange peel

Pour liquid ingredients into an ice-filled shaker. Shake, then strain into a cocktail glass. Squeeze a twist of orange peel on top.

IDEAL

2 ounces gin
1 ounce sweet vermouth
3 dashes maraschino
Splash grapefruit juice

Pour liquid ingredients into an ice-filled shaker. Shake, then strain into a cocktail glass.

SENSATION

3 ounces gin
1 ounce lemon juice
3 dashes maraschino
3 sprigs mint

Pour liquid ingredients into an ice-filled shaker. Shake, then strain into a cocktail glass. Garnish with mint.

RUM DRINKS

HONOLULU COOLER

3 ounces amber rum
1 teaspoon powdered sugar
Juice of 1 lime
2 dashes raspberry syrup

Pour liquid ingredients into an ice-filled shaker. Shake, then strain into a cocktail glass.

EL CHICO

A favorite in the 1940s at El Chico restaurant in Greenwich Village.

1½ ounces amber rum
½ ounce sweet vermouth
Dash grenadine
Dash curaçao
Maraschino cherry
Twist of lemon

Pour liquid ingredients into an ice-filled shaker. Shake, then strain into a cocktail glass. Add cherry and lemon twist.

ISLE OF PINES

3 ounces light rum
Dash grapefruit juice
Squeeze of lime juice

Pour ingredients into an ice-filled shaker. Shake, then strain into a cocktail glass.

DAIQUIRI *

2 ounces white or amber
  rum
Juice of ½ lime
1 teaspoon superfine sugar

Pour ingredients into an ice-filled shaker. Shake, then strain into a cocktail glass.

PIÑA COLADA *

2 ounces amber rum
2 ounces coconut cream
4 ounces pineapple juice
Pineapple stick
Maraschino cherry

Shake liquid ingredients in an ice-filled shaker, or blend with ice in a blender. Strain into an ice-filled highball glass, garnish with pineapple stick and cherry.

DARK AND STORMY

1 ½ ounces Gosling's Black
  Seal rum
4 ounces ginger beer
Lemon or lime wedge

Pour rum over ice in a tall glass, top up with ginger beer, squeeze in a lemon or lime wedge.

BERMUDA ANGLER

Created in the 1930s by E. F. Warner, then the publisher of *Field and Stream*.

---

2 ounces amber rum
1 ounce lime juice
1 teaspoon Cointreau

Pour ingredients into an ice-filled shaker. Shake, then strain into a cocktail glass.

BETWEEN THE SHEETS

½ ounce light rum
½ ounce brandy
½ ounce lemon juice
½ ounce curaçao

Pour ingredients into an ice-filled shaker. Shake, then strain into a cocktail glass.

SANS SOUCI COOLER

Courtesy Sans Souci Hotel, Ocho Rios, Jamaica

---

1 ounce amber rum
1 ½ ounces pineapple juice
½ ounce orange juice
½ ounce simple syrup
Dash lime juice
Wedge of pineapple and
    orange, for garnish
Maraschino cherry, for
    garnish

Pour liquid ingredients into an ice-filled shaker, shake, then strain into a tall glass. Garnish with a wedge of pineapple, a wedge of orange, and a cherry.

JAMAICA SWIZZLE

1½ ounces Jamaica rum
Juice of 1 lime
1 teaspoon fine granulated
  sugar
6 dashes Angostura bitters

Pour ingredients into a glass pitcher, add plenty of shaved ice, churn with a swizzle stick until pitcher frosts. Strain into a cocktail glass and serve.

WASHINGTON COCKTAIL

Courtesy Fraunces Tavern, New York City

1½ ounces Myers's dark
  rum
½ ounce gin
Splash Cointreau
½ ounce lemon juice
Splash orange juice
1 tablespoon sugar
Maraschino cherry

Pour ingredients except maraschino cherry into an ice-filled shaker. Shake, then strain into a cocktail glass. Garnish with cherry.

EL FLORIDITA DAIQUIRI *

1¾ ounces white rum
Juice of 1 lime
2 teaspoons sugar syrup
Splash maraschino

Pour liquid ingredients into an ice-filled shaker. Shake, then strain into a cocktail glass.

159

KEVIN'S MANGO COLADA

Courtesy Mango's, Anguilla, B.W.I.

1 ounce white rum
1 ounce cream of coconut
1 ounce mango juice
2 slices ripe mango
Dash Cointreau
Dash vanilla extract
Sprinkling of cinnamon

Blend all ingredients in an electric blender with ½ cup ice until thick and smooth, then pour into a large glass.

PLANTERS PUNCH

1¼ ounces Myers's rum
3 ounces orange juice
Juice of ½ lemon
1 teaspoon sugar
Dash grenadine
Orange slice
Maraschino cherry

Pour rum, orange and lemon juice, sugar, and grenadine into an ice-filled shaker. Shake, then strain into a tall glass with ice. Add orange slice and cherry.

EL PRESIDENTE

1 ounce white rum
½ ounce curaçao
½ ounce dry vermouth
Dash grenadine

Pour ingredients into an ice-filled shaker. Shake, then strain into a cocktail glass.

KOALKEEL BOMB

Courtesy Koalkeel Restaurant, Anguilla, B.W.I.

1 ounce dark rum
2 ounces brandy
1 ounce lime juice
1 ounce simple syrup
½ ounce crème de cassis

Pour ingredients into an ice-filled shaker. Shake, then strain into a cocktail glass.

BOLO

2 ounces white or amber rum
Juice of ½ lime
Juice of ¼ orange
1 teaspoon sugar

Pour ingredients into an ice-filled shaker. Shake, then strain into a cocktail glass.

MOJITO *

Juice of ½ lime
1 teaspoon sugar
Mint leaves
2 ounces white rum
4 ounces club soda
(optional)

Place lime juice and sugar in a highball glass and stir until sugar is dissolved. Add a few mint leaves, pressing them against the side of the glass. Fill with crushed ice. Add the rum. Top up with soda (optional), garnish with a sprig of mint.

CHAMPAGNE DRINKS

PARK AVENUE

From *The Stork Club Bar Book* (1946)

1 ounce brandy
½ ounce Grand Marnier
4 ounces chilled champagne

Pour brandy and Grand Marnier into a champagne glass over a cube of ice. Top up with champagne and serve.

THE PICK-ME-UP

Created in 1962 by Georges Melitz of the Ritz, Paris

2 ounces orange juice
1 ounce brandy
1 ounce Cointreau
4 ounces champagne

Pour orange juice, brandy, and Cointreau into an ice-filled shaker. Shake, strain into a mixing glass, and top up with champagne.

PRINTER'S ROW

Courtesy Printer's Row Restaurant, Chicago

4 ounces champagne
¼ ounce Clément Créole
Mint leaf

Pour the Clément Créole into a champagne flute. Add champagne, and twist in the mint leaf. Note: Too much Créole will flatten the champagne.

GEORGE V

Courtesy Le Titi de Paris, Arlington Heights, Illinois

⅓ ounce liqueur de fraise
5 ounces champagne
I teaspoon Cointreau
Orange slice

Pour liqueur de fraise into bottom of champagne flute. Slowly pour in champagne and top with Cointreau poured slowly over the back of a spoon. Garnish with orange slice squeezed into cocktail.

POUSSE RAPIÈRE

Courtesy L'Impromptu Restaurant, Montreal

½ ounce Pousse Rapière
(Armagnac-orange
liqueur)
4 ounces champagne
Orange peel

Pour the Pousse Rapière in a champagne flute, top up with champagne, and garnish with long, spiral tendrils of orange peel.

CHAMPAGNE COCKTAIL

I cube sugar
Angostura bitters
3 ounces chilled champagne
Twist of lemon

Place the sugar cube in a champagne glass and moisten it with a dash or two of Angostura bitters. Add champagne and garnish with a twist of lemon.

CHAMPEARMINT

Courtesy Jean-Luc Deguines, Mark Hotel, New York City

1 ounce Massenez Poire William (or other pear brandy)
1 dash vodka
4 ounces chilled champagne
Slice of fresh pear
2 fresh mint leaves
Dash white crème de menthe

Add brandy and vodka to a chilled champagne flute, then top up with champagne. Garnish with a slice of pear and two fresh mint leaves. Pour a dash of crème de menthe over the pear slice.

LE PERROQUET

Courtesy Le Perroquet, Chicago

Generous dash Campari
Dash gin
2 ounces orange juice
4 ounces champagne
Lemon and orange peel

Pour Campari, gin, and orange juice into a champagne flute, then top up with champagne. Garnish with a twist of lemon and orange.

VODKA DRINKS

LEMON VODKA MARTINI

2 ounces lemon vodka
2 to 3 drops Cointreau
Twist of lemon

Pour vodka and Cointreau into an ice-filled shaker. Shake, then strain into a martini glass. Serve with a twist of lemon.

SALTY DOG

Lime wedge
Salt and sugar, mixed, to
   coat rim of glass
2 ounces vodka
4 ounces grapefruit juice

Moisten the rim of an old-fashioned glass with lime wedge, then roll the rim in a mixture of equal parts salt and sugar. Fill glass with ice cubes, add vodka and grapefruit juice, and stir.

BRISTOL MARTINI

1¾ ounces lemon-flavored
   vodka
1 drop Cointreau
Twist of lemon

Courtesy Bristol Lounge, Four Seasons Hotel, Boston

Pour vodka and Cointreau into an ice-filled shaker. Shake, then strain into a cocktail glass. Add lemon twist.

JALAPEÑO BLOODY BULL

Courtesy Michael's Restaurant, Santa Monica, California

(for 6 servings)

1–3 fresh jalapeño peppers
Large red bell pepper, quartered
Large bunch fresh cilantro
5 ounces Worcestershire sauce
1 tablespoon freshly ground black pepper
Dash or 2 Tabasco
Salt
6 cups tomato juice
1½ cups vodka
1½ cups beef consommé
6 stalks celery stalks
3 limes, quartered
Fresh jalapeño pepper, sliced crossways, for garnish (optional)

A day ahead, quarter 1 or 2 jalapeños (depending on how hot you want the drinks to be) and the bell pepper—seeds, stems, and all—into a large glass jar or pitcher, along with the cilantro, Worcestershire sauce, black pepper, Tabasco, and salt to taste. Add the tomato juice, cover the jar, and refrigerate for 24 hours.

Before serving, pour the juice through a sieve to remove the solids.

Fill six 12-ounce glasses with ice cubes. Pour 2 ounces vodka and 2 ounces beef consommé into each glass. Top off each glass with the tomato juice mixture. Add a celery stalk to each glass and use it to stir up the drink slightly. Add 2 lime quarters to each glass, squeezing them as you put them in. If you like, slice another jalapeño for garnish.

GREEN EYE-OPENER

Courtesy Sign of the Dove, New York

1½ ounces vodka
Dash Rose's lime juice
2 ounces orange juice
Dash blue curaçao
Dash Cointreau
Celery stalk

Shake liquid ingredients with ice and serve in a tall glass with a stalk of celery.

BLOODY MARY *

3 ounces pepper vodka
4 ounces V-8 juice
Juice of lemon wedge
Juice of lime wedge
Dash of Worcestershire sauce
Pinch celery salt
Salt and pepper
Celery stalk

Pour liquid ingredients over ice and stir. (I prefer the slow, steady fire of Stolichnaya's Pertsovka vodka, but Absolut Peppar has a fresh jalapeño and green-chili zing that makes for a kind of Tex-Mex Bloody Mary.) Add celery salt, salt and pepper to taste, and stir with a celery stalk.

THE BLOOMS

3 ounces vodka
4 ounces tomato juice
1/4 teaspoon horseradish
1/8 teaspoon Dijon mustard
1/8 teaspoon Tabasco
Juice of 1 lemon
Pinch Old Bay seasoning
Salt and pepper

Second Prize, Stolichnaya New York State Bloody Mary Mix-Off, 1989

Pour liquid ingredients into an ice-filled collins glass and stir. Add seasonings and stir again.

VODKA GIMLET

Philip Marlowe, Raymond Chandler's great detective, insisted that there is only one way to make a gimlet: equal parts vodka and Rose's. That's too sweet for modern tastes.

3 ounces vodka
1/2 ounce Rose's lime juice

Pour over ice in a short glass and stir.

SILVERADO

1 1/2 ounces vodka
1 1/2 ounces Campari
1 1/2 ounces orange juice

Pour ingredients over ice in a short glass and stir.

TEQUILA DRINKS

MARGARITA

Lime wedge
Salt
2 ounces tequila
½ ounce Cointreau
1 tablespoon lime juice

Rub the rim of a glass with the lime wedge, then dip rim in salt. Pour remaining ingredients into an ice-filled shaker, shake, then strain into salt-rimmed glass.

TEQUILA SUNRISE

1½ ounces tequila
¾ ounce grenadine
4 ounces orange juice

Pour ingredients into an ice-filled shaker. Shake, then strain into a cocktail glass.

ARIZONA LEMONADE

Courtesy Arizona 206, New York City

2 ounces high-quality gold
  tequila
8 ounces fresh lemonade,
  slightly sweet
Lemon wheel or wedge

Pour liquid ingredients into a tall, ice-filled glass. Garnish with lemon.

RED HOT RITA

Courtesy Arizona 206, New York City

2 ounces jalapeño-flavored
  tequila
1 ounce Cointreau
1 ounce fresh-squeezed
  lime juice
Lime wedge
Small jalapeño pepper

Mix liquid ingredients and shake with ice; serve in a 6-ounce glass. Garnish with lime and jalapeño pepper.

WINE AND VERMOUTH COCKTAILS

VERMOUTH COCKTAIL

3 ounces dry vermouth
Dash Cointreau
2 dashes Angostura bitters
Twist of lemon

Pour liquid ingredients over ice in a short glass, add lemon twist.

VERMOUTH CASSIS

3 ounces dry vermouth
1 ounce crème de cassis
Club soda
Twist of lemon

In a tall glass filled with ice, combine vermouth and crème de cassis. Top up with soda and garnish with lemon twist.

CORONATION

Second Prize, *Police Gazette*, 1903

3½ ounces dry sherry
½ ounce French vermouth
Dash maraschino
Dash orange bitters
Olive
Twist of lemon

Pour liquid ingredients into an ice-filled shaker. Shake, then strain into a glass. Add olive and lemon twist.

WHITE PORT COCKTAIL

Cheap California versions have given white port an undeserved bad name. Try Burmester's Dry Chip.

3 ounces dry white port
Twist of lemon

Pour port into an ice-filled cocktail glass. Garnish with lemon twist.

BAMBOO

2 ounces dry sherry
¾ ounce dry vermouth
Dash orange bitters

Stir ingredients well with cracked ice. Strain into a 3-ounce cocktail glass.

ADONIS

Named after the first Broadway musical to run for more than 500 performances. The show opened at the Bijou Opera House on September 9, 1884. The cocktail was a standard at the bar of the old Waldorf.

1½ ounces dry sherry
½ ounce sweet vermouth
2 dashes orange bitters (or
    twist of orange)

Pour liquid ingredients into an ice-filled shaker. Shake, then strain into a cocktail glass. Add orange twist if using instead of bitters.

MISCELLANEOUS

AMERICANO

1 ounce Campari
½ ounce sweet vermouth
Club soda
Orange slice

Pour Campari and sweet vermouth over ice cubes in a short glass and top up with soda. Garnish with an orange slice.

JEFFERSON PIMM'S CUP

Courtesy Jefferson Hotel, Washington, D.C.

Pimm's No. 1 Cup
7-Up
Club soda
Sprig of mint
Slice of cucumber
Orange peel
Maraschino cherry

Fill a tall ice-filled glass with equal parts Pimm's No. 1 Cup, 7-Up, and club soda. Stir and garnish with a mint sprig, a cucumber slice, orange peel, and a maraschino cherry.

VENETIAN SUNSET

Courtesy Sam Peros, bartender, Felidia Restaurant, New York

1 ounce grappa
2 ounces fresh orange juice
Dash Campari

Pour ingredients into an ice-filled shaker. Shake, then pour into a martini glass.

PARLOR PUNCH

From Lafcadio Hearn's *La Cuisine Créole* (1885)

6 ounces English black tea
3 ounces whiskey
1½ ounces Jamaica rum
1 tablespoon sugar
Dash lemon juice
Dash raspberry syrup

Pour ingredients into an ice-filled shaker. Shake, then strain into a cocktail glass.

THE UNEXPECTED

Courtesy Basil's Bar and Restaurant, Mustique, B.W.I.

1 ounce Cointreau
Squeeze of lime or lemon
    juice
4 ounces club soda

Pour Cointreau and lime or lemon juice into an ice-filled highball glass and top up with soda.

ROSALIND RUSSELL

Contributed to *The Stork Club Bar Book* (1946) by the actress

2 ounces aquavit
1 ounce dry vermouth or
    blond Dubonnet

Pour ingredients into an ice-filled shaker. Shake, then strain into a cocktail glass.

CASSIS HIGHBALL

1 ounce crème de cassis
2 dashes Angostura bitters
4 ounces club soda

Pour the cassis into an ice-filled highball glass and add the bitters. Top up with soda and stir.

NONALCOHOLIC DRINKS

LIME RICKEY

1 tablespoon Rose's lime
  juice
Club soda
Twist of lime

Pour Rose's lime juice into an ice-filled high-ball glass and top up with club soda. Serve with a twist of lime.

GRAPEFRUIT COOLER

2 ounces grapefruit juice
Splash grenadine
4 ounces club soda

Add the grapefruit juice and grenadine to an ice-filled highball glass, stir, then top up with soda.

AMANPURI

2 ounces pineapple juice
3 ounces orange juice
2 ounces passion fruit juice
2 ounces pink grapefruit
  juice
1 dash grenadine
1 tablespoon lemon mix
  (equal parts lemon bitter,
  egg white, sugar syrup)
¼ slice orange

Courtesy Jean-Luc Deguines, Mark Hotel, New York City

Pour ingredients into an ice-filled shaker, shake, then strain into a collins glass. Garnish with an orange slice.

ANGOSTURA COCKTAIL

1 cube sugar
2–3 dashes Angostura
  bitters
4 ounces club soda
Twist of lemon

Place the sugar cube in the bottom of a short ice-filled glass and soak it with the bitters. Add soda and serve with a lemon twist.

RHUBARB HIGHBALL

2 cups sugar
3 cups diced rhubarb
Orange juice
Club soda
Sprig of mint

Mix the sugar with a cup of water, heat in a double boiler, and add rhubarb just before the water boils. Simmer until tender, then rub through a sieve and mix with an equal part of orange juice. Fill ice-filled highball glass two thirds full of the rhubarb–orange juice mixture, top up with soda, and garnish with mint sprig. Serves 4.

BIBLIOGRAPHY

Adams, Ramon. *Western Words*. Norman, Okla.: University of Oklahoma Press, 1968.

Ade, George. *The Old-Time Saloon*. New York: R. Long & R. R. Smith, 1931.

Altschul, Ira D. *Drinks as They Were Made Before Prohibition*. Santa Barbara, Cal.: Schauer Printing Studio, 1934.

Amis, Kingsley. *On Drink*. London: Jonathan Cape, 1972.

Arthur, Stanley Clisby. *Famous New Orleans Drinks and How to Mix 'Em*. New Orleans: Harmanson, 1937.

Asbury, Herbert, ed. *The Bon Vivant's Companion, or How to Mix Drinks*, by Professor Jerry Thomas. New York: Knopf, 1928.

Baker, Charles H., Jr. *The Gentleman's Companion. Vol. 1, Being an Exotic Drinking Book*. New York: Crown, 1946.

Barkeepers' Ready Reference. St. Louis: A. V. Bevill, 1871.

Bartender's Guide: How to Mix Drinks. Milwaukee: Royal, 1914.

Bartlett, John Russell. *Dictionary of Americanisms*, 4th ed. Boston: Little, Brown, 1877.

Barty-King, Hugh, and Anton Massel. *Rum: Yesterday and Today*. London: Heinemann, 1983.

Bayles, W. Harrison. *Old Taverns of New York*. New York: Frank Allaben Genealogical Co., 1915.

Beebe, Lucius. *The Stork Club Bar Book*. New York: Rinehart, 1946.

Bergeron, Victor J. *Trader Vic's Bartender's Guide*. Garden City, N.Y.: Doubleday, 1972.

Berrey, Lester V., and Melvin van den Bark. *The American Thesaurus of Slang*, 2nd ed. New York: Crowell, 1953.

Birmingham, Frederic A., ed. *Esquire Drink Book*. New York: Harper & Brothers, 1956.

Boothby, William T. *Cocktail Boothby's American Bartender*. San Francisco: San Francisco News Co., 1891.

Bridenbaugh, Carl. *Cities in the Wilderness: The First Century of Urban Life in America, 1625–1742*. New York: Ronald Press, 1938.

———. *Cities in Revolt: Urban Life in America, 1743–1776*. New York: Knopf, 1955.

Brooks, Johnny. *My 35 Years Behind Bars*. New York: Exposition Press, 1954.

Brown, John Hull. *Early American Beverages*. Rutland, Vt.: C. E. Tuttle, 1966.

Buñuel, Luis. *My Last Sigh*. New York: Vintage, 1984.

Byron, O. H. *The Modern Bartenders' Guide*. New York: Excelsior, 1884.

Carson, Gerald. *The Social History of Bourbon*. New York: Dodd, Mead, 1963.

Chayette, Hervé, and Alain Weill. *Les cocktails*. Paris: Editions Nathan, 1988.

Conrad, Barnaby, III. *Absinthe*. San Francisco: Chronicle Books, 1988.

Craddock, Harry. *The Savoy Cocktail Book*. London: Constable & Co., 1930.

Crahan, Marcus. *Early American Inebrietatis*. Los Angeles: Zamorano Club, 1964.

Craigie, Sir William A. *A Dictionary of American English on Historical Principles*, vols. 1–4. Chicago: University of Chicago Press, 1959.

Crockett, Albert Stevens. *The Old Waldorf-Astoria Bar Book*. New York: Dodd, Mead, 1934.

———. *Old Waldorf Bar Days*. New York: Aventine Press, 1931.

Crowgey, Henry G. *Kentucky Bourbon: The Early Years of Whiskey Making*. Lexington: University of Kentucky Press, 1972.

Dabney, Joseph Earl. *Mountain Spirits*. New York: Scribners, 1974.

De Gouy, Louis P. *The Cocktail Hour*. New York: Greenberg, 1951.

DeVoto, Bernard. *The Hour*. Boston: Riverside Press, 1948.

Dorchester, Daniel. *The Liquor Problem in All Ages*. New York: Phillips and Hunt, 1888.

Doxat, John. *Stirred—Not Shaken: The Dry Martini*. London: Hutchinson Benham, 1976.

———. *The World of Drinks and Drinking*. New York: Drake, 1972.

Duffy, Patrick Gavin. *The Official Mixer's Manual*. New York: R. Long & R. R. Smith, 1934.

Durrell, Edward Henry ("Henry Didimus"). *New Orleans As I Found It*. New York, Harper & Brothers, 1845.

Earle, Alice M. *Customs and Fashions in Old New England*. New York, Scribner's, 1902.

———. *Home Life in Colonial Days*. New York: Macmillan, 1906.

———. *"Old Colonial Drinks and Drinkers." National Magazine* 16 (June 1892).

———. *Stage-coach and Tavern Days*. New York: Macmillan, 1900.

Edmunds, Lowell. *The Silver Bullet: The Martini in American Civilization*. Westport, Conn.: Greenwood Press, 1981.

Edwards, Bill. *How to Mix Drinks*. Philadelphia: David McKay, 1936.

Embury, David A. *The Fine Art of Mixing Drinks*. Garden City, N.Y.: Doubleday, 1948.

Emerson, Edward R. *Beverages Past and Present*, vols. 1–2. New York: Putnam's, 1908.

Engel, Leo. *American and Other Drinks*. London: Tinsley Bros., 1880.

Esquire's Handbook for Hosts. New York: Grosset & Dunlap, 1949.

Farmer, John S. *Americanisms—Old and New*. London: Th. Poulter, 1889.

Feery, William C. *Wet Drinks for Dry People*. Chicago: Bazner Press, 1932.

Field, Edward. *The Colonial Tavern*. Providence, R.I.: Preston and Rounds, 1897.

Field, S. S. *The American Drink Book*. New York, Farrar, Straus and Young, 1953.

Fleischmann, Joseph. *The Art of Blending and Compounding Liquors and Wines*. Danbury, Conn.: Behrens, 1885.

Fougner, G. Selmer. *Along the Wine Trail*, vols. 1–5. New York: New York Sun, 1934–36. Contains reprinted columns, many of them on cocktails, written for the *New York Sun*.

———. *Baron Fougner's Bar Guide*. Detroit: n.p., 1940.

Furnas, J. C. *The Life and Times of the Late Demon Rum*. New York: Putnam's, 1965.

Gaige, Crosby. *Crosby Gaige's Cocktail Guide and Lady's Companion*. New York: M. Barrows, 1941.

———. *The Standard Cocktail Guide*. New York: M. Barrows, 1944.

Giggle Water. New York: Ch. S. Warnock, 1928.

Gorman, Marion, and Felipe P. de Alba. *The Tequila Book*. Chicago: Regnery, 1976.

Grohusko, Jacob. *Jack's Manual*. New York: Knopf, 1933.

Guyer, William, ed. *The Merry Mixer*. New York: J. E. Pepper, 1933.

Haimo, Oscar. *Cocktail and Wine Digest*. New York: n.p., 1945.

Hall, Basil. *Travels in North America in the Years 1827 and 1828*, vols. 1–3. Edinburgh, 1829.

Haney, Jesse. *Haney's Steward and Barkeeper's Manual*. New York: Jesse Haney, 1869.

Harwell, Richard B. *The Mint Julep*. Charlottesville: University Press of Virginia, 1975.

Haywood, Joseph L. *Mixology: The Art of Preparing All Kinds of Drinks*. Wilmington: Press of the Sunday Star, 1898.

Hemingway, Ernest. *Islands in the Stream*. New York: Scribners, 1970.

Herzbrun, Robert. *The Perfect Martini Book*. New York: Harcourt Brace Jovanovich, 1979.

Hoffmann, Henry. *The "Count" Reminisces*. St. Louis: Hoffmann and Kurz, 1933.

Holbrook, Stewart H. *Far Corner: A Personal View of the Pacific Northwest*. New York: Macmillan, 1952.

Hooker, Richard J. *Food and Drink in America*. Indianapolis: Bobbs Merrill, 1981.

Janson, Charles William. *The Stranger in America, 1793–1806*. New York: Press of the Pioneers, 1935.

Jillson, Willard Rouse. *Early Kentucky Distillers*. Louisville: Standard Printing, 1940.

Johnson, Byron A., and Sharon Peregrine Johnson. *Wild West Bartenders' Bible*. Austin: Texas Monthly Press, 1986.

Johnson, Harry. *Bartender's Manual*. New York: Samisch & Goldmann, 1882.

Kappeler, George J. *Modern American Drinks*. New York: Merriam, 1895.

Keller, Mark, and Mairi McCormick. *A Dictionary of Words About Alcohol*. New Brunswick, N.J.: Publications Division, Rutgers Center of Alcohol Studies, 1968.

Kobler, John. *Ardent Spirits: The Rise and Fall of Prohibition*. New York: G. P. Putnam's, 1973.

Krout, John A. *The Origins of Prohibition*. New York: Knopf, 1925.

Lamore, Harry. *The New Police Gazette Bartenders Guide*. New York: Richard K. Fox, 1901.

Lawlor, Christopher F. *The Mixologist*. Cincinnati: R. Clarke, 1895.

Lender, Mark Edward, and James Kirby Martin. *Drinking in America*. New York: Free Press, 1982.

McCusker, John J. *Rum and the American Revolution*. New York: Garland, 1989.

MacElhone, Harry. *Barflies and Cocktails*. Paris: Lecram Press, 1927.

———. *Harry's ABC of Mixing Cocktails*. London: Souvenir Press, 1986. First published 1919.

Marryat, Frederick. *A Diary in America*. Bloomington: Indiana University Press, 1968.

Meier, Frank. *The Artistry of Mixing Drinks*. Paris: Fryam Press, 1936.

Mencken, Henry L. *The American Language*. New York: Knopf, 1937; Supplement I (1945); Supplement II (1948).

———. *Happy Days*. New York: Knopf, 1940.

———. *Tall Tales and Hoaxes of H. L. Mencken*. Ed. John W. Baer. Annapolis: Franklin Printing, 1990.

Michaux, François André. *Travels to the Westward of the Allegheny Mountains*. London: J. Mawman, 1805.

Montague, Harry. *The Up-to-Date Bartender's Guide*. Ottenheimer, 1913.

Monzert, Leonard. *The Independent Liquorist*. New York: Dick & Fitzgerald, 1866.

Mueller, Charles C. *Pioneers of Mixing*. New York: Trinity Press, 1934. Described on title page as "Collection of recipes from the log of American traveling mixicologists."

Noling, A. W. *Beverage Literature: A Bibliography*. Metuchen, N.J.: Scarecrow Press, 1971.

O'Hara, John. *Appointment in Samarra*. New York: Random House, 1934.

One Hundred Famous Cocktails. New York: Kenilworth Press, 1934. "Published in collaboration with Oscar of the Waldorf."

Peke, Hewson L. *Americana Ebrietatis*. New York, 1917.

Porter, Henry, and George Roberts. *Cups and Their Customs*. London, 1869.

Powner, Willard. *The Complete Bartender's Guide*. Chicago: Powner, 1934.

Proskauer, Julien J. *What'll You Have?* New York: A. L. Burt, 1934.

Rawling, Ernest P. *Rawling's Book of Mixed Drinks*. San Francisco: Guild Press, 1914.

Reibstein, August. *"Mixology": Recipes for Old and New Mixed Drinks*. New York: August Reibstein, 1933.

Reinhardt, Charles Nicholas. *"Cheerio!"* New York: Elf Publishing Co., 1928. Author identified as "Charles, formerly of Delmonico's."

Root, Waverley, and Richard de Rochemont. *Eating in America: A History*. New York: Ecco, 1981.

Rorabaugh, W. J. *The Alcoholic Republic: An American Tradition.* New York: Oxford University Press, 1979.

Schmidt, A. William ("The Only William"). *The Flowing Bowl.* New York: C. L. Webster, 1892.

Scientific Bar-Keeping. Buffalo, N.Y.: E. N. Cook, 1884.

Stuart, Thomas. *Stuart's Fancy Drinks and How to Mix Them.* New York: Excelsior, 1896.

Swan, Fred W. *When Good Fellows Get Together (Drink and Service Manual).* Chicago: Reilly & Lee, 1933.

Thomas, Jerry. *The Bar-tender's Guide.* New York: Dick & Fitzgerald, 1862.

Thornton, Richard H. *An American Glossary.* Philadelphia: J. B. Lippincott, 1912.

Torelli, Adolphe. *900 recettes de cocktails et boissons américaines.* Paris: S. Bornemann, 1930.

Townshend, Jack. *The Bartender's Book.* New York: Viking, 1951.

Valentine's Manual of Old New York. New York: Valentine's Manual, Inc., 1923, 1926, 1927.

Walker, Danton. *Guide to New York Night Life.* New York: G. P. Putnam's Sons, 1958.

Weiss. Harry. *The History of Applejack or Apple Brandy in New Jersey from Colonial Times to the Present.* Trenton, N.J.: New Jersey Agricultural Society, 1954.

West, Elliot. *The Saloon on the Rocky Mountain Mining Frontier.* Lincoln, Neb., 1979.

Willkie, H. F. *Beverage Spirits in America: A Brief History.* New York: Newcomen Society of England, American Branch, 1949.

Woon, Basil Dillon. *When It's Cocktail Time in Cuba.* New York: Liveright, 1928.

Worden, Helen. *Here Is New York.* New York: Doubleday, Doran & Co., 1939.

INDEX

Numbers in **bold type** refer to recipes.

Abbey, **147**
absinthe, 80, 83, 84, 85, 89, 90, 92, 136
Absolut vodka, 123–24
Acrelius, Isaac, 44–45, 46, 50
Ade, George, 72
Adonis, **172**
advertising, 116, 125–26
    vodka, 120, 123–24
    whiskey, 109, 112, 113
Affinity, **141**
Alexander, 103, 108
Algonquin, **139**
alicante, 38
"Along the Wine Trail" (Fougner), 21–22, 88, 142

Amanpuri, **176**
American Cookery (Simmons), 45
American Language, The (Mencken), 63
Americano, **173**
Anderson, Sherwood, 26
Angostura Cocktail, **177**
anti-fogmatic, 64
applejack, 42, 51, 107–8
apples, 40, 52, 76
Appointment in Samarra (O'Hara), 102
Approve, **141**
Aqua Velva Collins, 113
Arizona Lemonade, **170**
Armagnac Lilli, **144**
Aviation, **146**
Azores, 38, 39

Balance and Columbian Repository, 22,
  58–59
Bamboo, 91, **172**
Barbary Coast, **142**
Baron, **153**
bars, 22, 29, 58, 79, 82–83, 84, 90,
  109, 122, 125, 128, 129
  accoutrements of, 77, 96, 134
  American, in Europe, 17, 18, 98,
    105, 123, 143
  hotel, 17–18, 68, 69–71, 74, 99,
    121, 145, 147, 172
  see also saloons; speakeasies; taverns,
    colonial
bartenders, 22, 23, 24, 27–28, 30, 60–
  61, 76–83, 85, 89, 125, 128
  Europe and, 79, 82–83, 98, 123
  hotel, 17–18, 28, 69, 70, 71, 76,
    78–79, 87, 110–11, 123
  Prohibition and, 98, 103–4
  repertoire of, 79–83, 103, 111
  robot, 127
  saloon, 67, 69, 71, 72, 79
*Bar-tender's Guide: The Bon-Vivant's
  Companion* (Thomas), 27, 65, 80,
  81, 83
bastard, 38
Battering Ram, 122
Beauty Spot, **154**
Beebe, Lucius, 109
beer, 72, 74, 95, 106, 114, 129, 130
  colonial, 36–37, 39, 40, 45, 46, 49
Bergeron, Victor "Trader Vic," 109,
  116–17
Berkeley, William, 40
Bermuda Angler, **158**
Between the Sheets, 103, **158**
bittered sling, 59, 64, 66, 110
bitters, 27, 28, 51, 59–60, 64, 79, 83,
  85, 131
  Angostura, 30, 66, 86, 110
  orange, 80, 84, 86

Peychaud's, 62, 89, 136
Stoughton's, 60
black-strap, 46
Bloody Mary, 122–23, **167**
Blooms, The, **168**
Blue Blazer, 81–82
Blue Monday, 119
Bodeguita del Medio (Havana), 106
Bolo, **161**
bombo (bumbo), 46
Bond, James, 19–20, 118, 121, 149
Boston, Mass., 37–38, 39, 40, 42, 43,
  44, 65, 88
Bouguereau, Adolphe William, 69–70
bourbon, 52–58, 72, 84, 109, 116, 130
Bradford, William, 36
brandy, 17, 37, 46, 50, 55, 60, 65, 66,
  71, 80, 83, 111, **143–45**
  applejack, 42, 51, 107–8
  bitters and, 62
  French, 64, 68, 89
  Hennessy, 71
  peach, 40, 51, 68
  Pisco, 91
Bristol Martini, **165**
Bronx, 21, 25, 84, 87–88, 92, 93, 97,
  108, **148**
Bronx Terrace, **154**
Brooklyn, **140**
Brooks, Johnny, 103
brûlé, 90
Brut, 86
Bryan, William Jennings, 85, 88
Buñuel, Luis, 29–30
Butterfield 8 (O'Hara), 30
Button Punch, 91
Byron, O. H., 27

calibogus, 46
California, 27, 73, 78, 90–91, 109,
  116–17, 120–21
Calvados Cocktail, **144**

Camac, William, 48
Campden, **148**
canary, 38, 39, 50
Canary Islands, 38
Cape Codder, **117**
Carson, Gerald, 53
Cassis Highball, **175**
champagne, 39, 41, 50, 70, 71, 133,
    162–64
Champagne Cocktail, 18, 80, 107, **163**
Champearmint, **164**
Chartreuse, 83
cherry bounce, 46
Chicago, Ill., 33, 82, 96, 98–99
Chipman, Richard Manning, 61–62
cider royal, 45, 46
ciders, 41, 50, 65, 80
    applejack, 42, 51, 107–8
    colonial, 40–42, 45, 46
City Breeze, **151**
Civil War, 55, 70
Claudel, Paul, 17
Clay, Henry, 56–57
Clover Club, 88, 92, 108
Club Cocktails, 80
cobblers, 63, 64, 82
cock ale, 62–63
cocktail lounge, 68, 101
cocktail party, 19
cocktails, 15–24, 58–63, 72, 107–17,
    125–31
    American social style and, 18–19
    barroom etymology of, 60–61, 89
    classic, 18, 22, 23, 84–92, 107, 122,
        128–29
    definitions of, 22–23, 59–60, 66, 80
    European attitude toward, 17–18
    first known reference to, 58–59
    origin of term, 60–63
    post-Prohibition drinking habits and,
        107–13, 125, 129
    premixed, 80, 97

in Soviet Union, 121–22
    trends in, 114–17, 118–19, 128–31
    tropical, 116–17, 128–29
    World War II military, 113–14
    yuppies and, 128, 129, 130–31
cocktail shakers, 79, 82, 93, 96, 134
Cointreau, 33
Coke 'n' Oke, 117
colonists, 15, 19, 36–48, 49, 52, 58,
    65, 84–85, 96
    beer of, 36–37, 39, 40, 45, 46, 49
    ciders of, 40–42, 45, 46
    liquor made by, 39–43
    Puritan, 35, 36–38
    rum of, 42–43, 45, 46–48, 84–85
    taverns of, *see* taverns, colonial
    whiskey of, 49, 52
    wines imported by, 37–39, 46
Columbus, 86
Columbus, Christopher, 42
Common Market Cocktail, 17–18
Cooking of the Caribbean Islands
    (Wolfe), 104
Cooper, James Fenimore, 61
Coronation, **171**
Corpse Reviver, 82, 83
Corvelo, Calif., 73
Cowboy, 103
Cox, Jennings, 104
Craig, Elijah, 52–53
Crawford, Joan, 121
Cream Fizz, 108
Crèvecoeur, St. John de, 40
Crockett, Albert Stevens, 80, 87
Crowgey, Henry G., 53
Cuba Libre, 114
Cubanola, 103
Cuisine Créole, La (Hearn), 90, 140,
    174
Cups and Their Customs (Porter and
    Roberts), 83
curaçao, 17, 28, 83

Daiquiris, 23, 104–6, 107, 108, 128, **157, 159**
Dark and Stormy, **157**
Davis, Elmer, 101
Davis, John, 54
Depth Charge, **154**
DeVoto, Bernard, 35, 87–88, 108, 110
Dickens, Charles, 57, 65
Dictionary of Americanisms (Bartlett), 60, 80–81
distilling industry, 32, 80, 104, 109, 112–13, 115–16, 125–26
   vodka, 120, 123–24
di Taggia, Martini di Arma, 28
Dom Pérignon, 71
Don the Beachcomber, 109, 117
Dos Passos, John, 30
Dripped Absinthe Frappé, 89, 92
Duffy, Patrick Gavin, 76, 110–11, 112, 140
Duplex, 87
Durrell, Edward Henry, 60
Dutch gin (genever), 107

Edmunds, Lowell, 29, 30–31
El Chico, **156**
El Floridita, **159**
El Floridita bar (Havana), 104, 105, 106
El Presidente, 104, **160**
Emerson, Joseph, 44
Esquire, 28, 33, 107–8

Farewell to Arms, A (Hemingway), 31
Farmer, John S., 66
Farmers' Club (London), 48
fayal, 39
Fish House Punch, 47–48, **48**
Fitzgerald, F. Scott, 93, 96, 97, 98
Flame of Love, The, **148**
Flanagan, Betsy, 60–61
flip, 15, 46–47, 59

Fluffy Ruffles, 108
Fougner, G. Selmer, 21–22, 88, 142
France, 60, 62, 82–83, 89, 105, 123, 143
   brandy of, 64, 68, 69
   wines of, 28, 30, 39, 45, 80, 84
Frappé New Orleans à la Graham, 86
free lunch, 74
Free Silver Fizz, 88
French, 75, **149**
Fuzzy Navel, 16, 126–27

Galliano, 126
Garbo, Greta, 102
George V, **163**
gimlet, 122, **168**
gin, 46, 66, 76, 84, 87, 88, 94, 102, 114, 121, 122, 126, **146–55**
   Dutch (genever), 107
   in martini, 26, 27, 28, 30
   Old Tom, 27, 80, 81
   sloe, 17
gin and tonic, 110, 118, 122
Gin Buck, **146**
Gin Daisy, 92, **146**
Gin Fizz, 89, 90, **153**
   Ramos, 89, 90, **150**
ginger ale, 98, 102
ginger beer, 120
Gladstone, 79–80
Golden Dream, 126
Goldfish, 100
Gower, Jonathan, 44
Grapefruit Cooler, **176**
"Great American Cocktail, The" (Irwin), 13
Great Britain, 17–18, 37, 46, 48, 49, 50, 63, 67, 82–83, 119
   colonial wine taxes imposed by, 38–39
   martinis of, 26, 28, 30
Green Eye-Opener, **167**

grog, 45, 46, 64
Grund, Francis, 68, 76
Guinan, Texas, 97, 100

Hall, Basil, 54–55
Hall, Isaac, 43
Harrison, William Henry, 41
Harry's New York Bar (Paris), 105, 123, 143
Harvest Moon, 107–8
Harvey Wallbanger, 126
Harwell, Richard Barksdale, 55
Havana, Cuba, 103–6
Hawthorne, Nathaniel, 77
Health Resort, 122
Hearn, Lafcadio, 90, 140, 174
Hemingway, Ernest, 31, 104, 105–6
Herbsaint, 89, 136
Her Foot Is on the Brass Rail (Marquis), 101
Heublein Company, 80, 120
highball, 23, 108, 109, 111, 112, 114, 116
hippocras, 40–41
Hoffman House (New York), 28, 69–71, 79, 84, 87
Hoffman House Fizz, **153**
Honolulu Cooler, **156**
Hotchner, A. E., 105
hotels, 54, 67, 90
  bars of, 17–18, 68, 69–71, 74, 99, 121, 145, 147, 172
  bartenders of, 17–18, 28, 69, 70, 71, 76, 78–79, 87, 110–11, 123
Hour, The (DeVoto), 25, 87

ice, 48, 54, 65, 83, 134
Ideal, **155**
Irving, Washington, 57, 63
Irwin, Wallace, 13
Isle of Pines, **156**
Italian wines, 18, 26, 27, 28, 39

Jack Rose, 25, 91, 130, **144**
Jalapeño Bloody Bull, **166**
Jamaica Swizzle, **159**
James Bond Martini (Vesper), **149**
Janson, Charles William, 59
Japanese, 80
Jefferson, Thomas, 39, 51
Jefferson Pimm's Cup, **173**
Jell-O Shot, 23, 127
Jersey, 80
Jessel, George, 122–23
Johnson, Lucius, 104
Johnson, Samuel, 128
Jones, James, 113
Josselyn, John, 40
julep, derivation of term, 54
  see also Mint Julep
jungle juice, 114

Kentucky, 52–58, 64
Kentucky Bourbon (Crowgey), 53
Kentucky Derby, 55, 58
Kevin's Mango Colada, **160**
Kieft, Willem, 39
Kipling, Rudyard, 91
Knickerbocker Hotel (New York), 28
Knight, Sarah, 44
Knox, Thomas W., 91
Koalkeel Bomb, **161**
Kunett, Rudolph, 120

Laird, William, 41–42
LaRoe, Earl, 126
Lava Lamp, 127
Lemon Ginger Tea, **151**
Lemon Punch, **142**
Lemon Vodka Martini, **165**
Le Perroquet, **164**
Lighthouse, 122
Lime Rickey, **176**
loggerhead, 47
London, Jack, 80

madeira, 38, 39, 46, 76
Mai Tai, 116
malaga, 38, 39
Manhattan, 13, 23, 27, 48, 80, 81, 85–
    87, 91, 93, 97, 108, 109, 114,
    116, 128, **138**
    bourbon vs. rye in, 109
    origin of, 85–86
Manhattan Club (New York), 86, 92
Manhattan Cocktail à la Gilbert, 86
Manhattan Cooler à la McGregor, 86
Manhattan Transfer (Dos Passos), 30
Margarita, 129, **169**
Marlborough House (New York), 97, 100
Marquis, Don, 101
Marryat, Frederick, 54, 55, 64
Martin, John G., 120
Martinez, 27, 28
Martini, 13, 15, 21, 23–24, 25–35, 48,
    56, 80, 85, 87, 97, 114, 116, 119,
    128, **149**
    Bristol, **165**
    business class adoption of, 20, 31–32
    classic glass for, 29, 34
    dry, 28, 31–33, 84, 107, 118
    gin in, 26, 27, 28, 30
    James Bond (Vesper), **149**
    Lemon Vodka, **165**
    in literature, 29–31
    origin of, 26–28
    preparation of, 26, 29–30, 31–33, 93,
        108, 110
    sweet, 26, 27, 28, 84
    symbolism acquired by, 28–29, 31,
        33, 34
    variations on, 29–30, 33
    vermouth in, 26, 27, 28, 30, 31–33
    vodka, 20, 34–35, 121, 122, **165**
    young drinkers and, 33–34
Martini & Rossi vermouth, 26
Maryland, 50, 55
Mary Pickford, 104

Massachusetts, 36–38, 39, 40, 42, 43,
    44, 47, 50, 65, 88
Massachusetts Spy, 49, 64
Mather, Increase, 37
mead, 39, 45
Medford rum, 43
Mencken, H. L., 16, 63, 67, 68, 108
metheglin, 39, 46
Michaux, François André, 51
mimbo, 46
Mingot, Don Ramón Portas, 128
Mint Julep, 54–58, 64, 68, 76, 89, 92,
    106, **136–37**
Mint Julep à la Creole, **137**
Mojito, 106, **161**
Montepulciano, 39
Morgan, J. Pierpont, 87
morning eye-openers, 54, 64, 82
Morning Glory, 82, 83
Morris, Samuel, 47
Morton, Morton C., 33
Moscow Mule, 120
Mulhall, William F., 28, 71, 84, 85
My 35 Years Behind Bars (Brooks), 103

Naked Martini, The, 32
Negroni, **151**
Negus, 46, 80
New Orleans, La., 60, 62, 73, 74, 89–
    90, 136
New York, N.Y., 44, 73, 84–89
    hotels of, 28, 34, 38, 68, 69–71, 74,
        76, 78, 79, 80, 84, 87, 88, 91–92,
        93, 98, 99, 108, 110–11, 121,
        145, 147, 172
    Prohibition in, 96, 97–98, 99–100,
        103
New Yorker, **141**
New Yorker, 28–29
New York Sun, 21–22, 26, 79, 88, 142,
    145
New York Times, 31–32, 121

Nicky Finn, **143**
nightclubs, 97, 100, 127
noyau, 83

Occidental Hotel (San Francisco), 27
Official Mixer's Manual, The (Duffy), 76,
    110–11, 140
O'Hara, John, 30, 102
okolehao, 117
Old 1776 whiskey, 52
Old Absinthe House (New Orleans), 89
Old-Fashioned, 84, 87, 89, 92, **137**
Old-Fashioned Dutch, 107
Old Tom gin, 27, 80, 81
Old Waldorf Bar Days (Crockett), 87
Orange Blossom, 88, 92, 108, 122
orange juice, 47, 88–89
orgeat, 80, 81, 108, 116

Papa Dobles, **105**
Paris Exposition of 1867, 82–83
Park Avenue, **162**
Parlor Punch, **174**
Pavilion Hotel (Staten Island), 68, 76
peach brandy, 40, 51, 68
Peachtree Schnapps, 126
peachy, 40
Pennsylvania, 42, 47–48, 63, 64, 88
    stillhouses in, 50–51
Pepper, Elijah, 52
Pepper, James E., 52, 137
Pérez, Ramón Marrero "Poppa Mon-
    chito," 128–29
Perfect, 92, **147**
Perrier water, 31
perry, 40
Petiot, Fernand, 123
Peychaud, Antoine, 62, 63, 89, 136
Pick-Me-Up, The, **162**
Piña Colada, 128–29, **157**
Pink Lady, 108
pioneers, 49–66

drink terms of, 58–66
ice used by, 54, 65–66
whiskey of, 49–58
Pisco Punch, 91
Planters Punch, 107, **160**
Plaza Hotel (New York), 34, 92, 98,
    121, 145
Plimpton, 86
Police Gazette, 77, 171
Police Gazette cocktail, 135
Pom Pom, 108
port, 38, 39, 76
porter, 37
Porter, Henry, 83
Portuguese wines, 38
Pousse-Café, 108
Pousse l'Amour, **145**
Pousse Rapière, **163**
Powell, William, 32, 93–94
prices, 50, 63, 71, 74, 99, 100, 123
Printer's Row, **162**
Prohibition, 40, 68, 72, 74, 85, 88,
    91–92, 98–106, 109, 110, 126,
    128, 143
    drinking habits affected by, 95–97,
    101–3, 107–13, 115, 125, 129
    Eighteenth Amendment and, 94, 96,
    98–99, 101, 106
    Havana as refuge from, 103–6
    repeal of, 106
    Volstead Act and, 94, 96
    see also speakeasies
punch, 44, 45, 46, 47–48, 50, 58, 64,
    76, 80, 82, 90, 91, 107, **142,
    160**
Puritans, 35, 36–38

Quatorze, **150**
Queen Anne, 86

Racquet, 86
Ramos, Henry C., 90

Ramos Gin Fizz, 89, 90, **150**
Red Hot Rita, **170**
Remsen Cooler, **138**
Revolutionary War, 50, 52, 60, 61, 62
Rhubarb Highball, **177**
Ribailagua, Constantino, 105
Richelieu, Julio, 27
Riding Club, 86
Roberts, George, 83
Robotender, 127
Rob Roy, 88, **139**
Roosevelt, Franklin D., 30, 119
Rosalind Russell, **175**
Roughing It (Twain), 78
Royal, **140**
Royal Cup, **86**
rum, 39, 50, 54, 55, 80, 103, 104–6,
    109, 114, 116, 128–29, **156–61**
  colonial, 42–43, 44, 45, 46–48,
    84–85
  triangle trade and, 42
rum punch, 45, 47–48
Russian Cocktail, 119
rye whiskey, 50–51, 52, 53, 55, 72, 82,
    89, 102, 109, 111, 113, 130, 133

sack-posset, 46
Sala, George Augustus, 82–83
saloons, 67–75, 85, 90, 91, 94, 96, 101
  bartenders of, 67, 69, 71, 72, 79
  corner, 71–72, 75, 128
  decor of, 68–70, 71–72, 75
  free lunch of, 74
  Western, 67, 69, 72–73
  see also bars; bartenders; speak-easies;
    taverns, colonial
Salty Dog, **165**
Sam Ward, 86
San Francisco, Calif., 27, 73, 78, 90–
    91, 121
sangaree, 45–46, 76
Sans Souci Cooler, **158**

Savoy Cocktail Book, 119, 141, 146
Savoy Hotel (London), 17–18
Sazerac, 62, 89, **136**
Sazerac House (New Orleans), 89,
    136
Schenley Distillers, 32
Schiller, John B., 89
schnapps, 126–27
Scotch, 20, 23, 33, 53, 81–82, 101,
    109, 111, 116, 118, 130
scotchem, 42
Screaming Orgasm, 127
Screwdriver, 122
Seabreeze, 126
Seagram's, 109, 115, 125–26
Sensation, **155**
Sex on the Beach, 16
Shady Grove Cooler, **152**
sherry, 38, 39
sherry-cobbler, 63
Sidecar, 21, 25, 108, 130, **143**
Silk Panties, 126
Silverado, **168**
Silver Bullet, The (Edmunds), 29
Silver Fizz, 88, 92
Simmons, Amelia, 45
slings, 44, 46, 59, 64, 66, 76, 110
Slippery Nipple, 16, 126
smashes, 80, 82
Smirnoff vodka, 120, 124
Smithtown, 86
Sobol, Joseph, 97, 99
Social History of Bourbon (Carson),
    53
Solon, Johnny, 87
South Side Fizz, **152**
Soviet Union, 30, 119–22, 123, 129
Spain, 38, 45
speakeasies, 94, 95, 97–98, 99–101
  decor of, 99–100
  women in, 101
  see also bars; saloons

Spotswood, Alexander, 49
Spy, The (Cooper), 61
Stalin, Joseph, 30, 119
Star, 86, **145**
State in Schuylkill, 47–48
Staten Island, 39, 68, 76
"stinkibus," 43
Stokes, Edward S., 69–70
Stolichnaya vodka, 123, 126
Stone Fence, 63, 65
Stork Club, **147**
sugar syrup, 27, 28, 79, 81, 83, 135
Sweetheart, 108
syllabub, 45

taverns, colonial, 17, 43–48, 55, 58,
    64, 67, 106
  entertainment in, 43–44
Tea, Lemon Ginger, **151**
Teague, Walter Dorwin, 112
Teeny Weeny Woo Woo, 16, 126, 127
temperance movement, 21, 37, 44
tent, 38
tequila, 114, 128, 129, **169–70**
Tequila Sunrise, **169**
Thatcher, George, 52
"Thin Man" movies, 32, 93–94
Thin Red Line, The (Jones), 113
Thomas, Jerry, 27–28, 65, 78–79, 80,
    81–82, 83
Thorpe, George, 49, 52
Tilden, William J., 86
Timber Doodle, 65
Time, 34, 108
Tip and Tic, 81, 82
toddies, 60, 76
Tom Collins, 81, 113, 114, **152**
Trader Vic's, 109, 116–17
tumblers, use of, 77, 81–82
Turf Club, 84
Twain, Mark, 65, 78
"21" Club (New York), 97, 98

Unexpected, The, **175**

Van Buren, Martin, 41
Venetian Sunset, **174**
vermouth, 17, 26, 27, 28, 30, 31–33,
    80, 84, 111, **171–73**
Vermouth Cassis, 107, **171**
Vermouth Cocktail, 80, 84, **171**
Vesper (James Bond Martini), **149**
Villas, James, 33–34
Virginia, 39, 40, 49–50, 54–56, 61
Virginia Gentleman bourbon, 53
vodka, 108, 118–24, 125, **165–68**
  advertising of, 120, 123–24
  Martini, Lemon, **165**
  superpremium, 123
  young drinkers and, 122
Vodka Gimlet, **168**
Vodka Martini, 20, 34–35, 121, 122,
    165
Volga, 121

Waldorf Hotel (New York), 74, 80, 87,
    92, 99, 108, 147, 172
Ward 8, 22, 88, 107, **139**
Washington, D.C., 33, 104
Washington, George, 51, 106, 113
Washington Cocktail, **159**
water, 37, 50
  limestone, 57
Waugh, Alec, 18
Waugh, Evelyn, 18
West Indies, 42, 50
wheat, 50, 51, 52
whiskey, 27, 49–58, 66, 80, 83, 95,
    101–2, 110, 121, **135–42**
  advertising of, 109, 112, 113
  blended, 115–16
  bourbon, 52–58, 72, 84, 109, 116,
    130
  distillation of, 50
  national brands of, 109

post-Prohibition supplies of, 113, 114
rye, 50–51, 52, 53, 55, 72, 82, 89,
    102, 109, 111, 113, 130, 133
taxes on, 51–52
of Western saloons, 67, 72–73
Whiskey Collins, **138**
Whiskey Rebellion, 51–52
Whiskey Sour, 84, 92, 114, **140**
White Plush, 88–89
White Port Cocktail, **172**
White Witch, 117
Williams, Evan, 52
wine, 17, 20, 23, 33, 41, 49, 50, 64,
    95, 106, 129, 131, **171–72**
colonial importation of, 37–39, 46
French, 28, 30, 39, 45, 80, 84
Rhine, 71

wine buyers, 71
Winthrop, John, 37
Winthrop, John, Jr., 40
Wolfe, Linda, 104
women, 44, 101
Wood, William, 37
World War I, 70
World War II, 30, 113–14, 116, 117,
    118, 119
wormwood (*Artemisia absinthium*), 85

Yale College, 38–39, 88
York, 80
yuppies, 128, 129, 130–31

Zaza, 21
Zombie, 109

ABOUT THE AUTHOR

William Grimes, formerly a contributor to *Esquire*'s "The Drinking Man" column and executive editor of *Avenue* magazine, first encountered the world of sophisticated drinking in the form of a quart of Ripple at Indiana University, where he majored in English. He went on to better wine and more degrees at the University of Chicago, from which he holds a Ph.D. in Comparative Literature. He is currently a culture reporter for the *New York Times* and lives in Astoria, New York, with his wife, Nancy.